Dennis McKenzie is an internationally renowned clairvoyant and psychic. Since he started working as a psychic, Dennis has put many grieving relatives in touch with their departed loved ones as well as offering all manner of wise words and advice on what the future holds.

Being the Soham Psychic

DENNIS McKENZIE
with Ellee Seymour

headline

First published in 2009
by HEADLINE PUBLISHING GROUP

1

Cataloguing in Publication Data is available from the British Library

ISBN 978 0 7553 1903 9

Typeset in Dante by Ellipsis Books Limited, Glasgow

Printed and bound in Great Britain by
Clays Ltd, St Ives plc

Headline's policy is to use papers that are natural,
renewable and recyclable products and made from wood grown
in sustainable forests. The logging and manufacturing processes
are expected to conform to the environmental regulations
of the country of origin.

HEADLINE PUBLISHING GROUP
An Hachette UK Company
338 Euston Road
London NW1 3BH

www.headline.co.uk
www.hachette.co.uk
www.dennismckenzie.com

*To Kevin and Nicola Wells, Mary Kelly and
to my grandkids, Sky-Lucy, Raegan-Lillie, Ashton,
Taye and Max – the lights of my life.*

There are so many people to acknowledge. Ellee Seymour helped turn my memories into words. At Headline I would like to thank Carly Cook who was a wise and supportive editor from beginning to end, and Josh Ireland for all his patience, and I can't write these acknowledgements without mentioning my PA, Judith, who makes everything possible. However, more than anything I am grateful to the many people who have let me share in their lives, and help them at their lowest points. They are the people who make having my gift worthwhile.

Prologue

'I am really sorry, but both the girls are dead.'

I knew within twenty-four hours of their disappearance that ten-year-old Holly Wells and Jessica Chapman had been murdered. But it wasn't until I met Holly's father and mother, three days after the girls had vanished without trace, that I would speak the words no parent should ever have to hear.

Kevin and Nicola Wells had insisted on the truth, however dreadful, and I delivered the verdict in my customary manner – bluntly and to the point. It is the only way I know. I spoke with total conviction; my German spirit guide, Jagna, had informed me, and Jagna is never wrong. There was something about the tone of her voice that told me that those girls had died in a terrible manner, she didn't need to say anything more for me to know that their deaths were more than just a tragic accident.

It broke my heart to have to tell the couple, clinging on to their last shred of hope, that they would never see their daughter again. That side of the job never gets easier, being the person to extinguish the hope.

Ten more days would pass before the two girls' bodies were found and what I had told Holly's parents would be confirmed: this included descriptions of the school care-taker, Ian Huntley, who would be convicted for the murder of both children, and of Huntley's girlfriend, Maxine Carr, who lied about his whereabouts on the night that he killed Holly and Jessica.

I had also described a view from the house Huntley shared with Carr, Huntley's red Ford Fiesta, the Fenland road he drove along to dispose of his victims' bodies and the site where he dumped them.

The spiritual encounters I shared with Kevin and Nicola Wells provided much comfort during that lowest point of their lives. They found solace in our three-way conversations with the spirit world: Holly would tell her mum how much she missed their shopping trips to Next and she would console her dad, too – she could see him sitting on her bed, crying, heartbroken, clutching her favourite cuddly toy.

My experience with the Wells family and so many others who have found themselves in the same tragic situation has made me realize that, however devastating it is to contact a child who has passed over in a brutal way, there is an absolute joy, real and heartrending, when the family are put in touch with the spirit of their loved one on the other side and they regain contact with someone they thought they would never speak to again. If what I do helps these people in any way, I can call myself blessed. Kevin and Nicola know that Holly has not gone. They know she's in a different place, but she's still watching. They know Holly is still around.

First Spiritual Encounters

I was four years old when I first saw her. I was in hospital following a terrible accident which left me in excruciating pain. Lots of nurses were looking after me but I couldn't help noticing that the nurse with the kind face who sat by my bed each night looked very different from the others. Her royal blue uniform with its starched white collar and long, full skirt seemed old-fashioned and she wore a tall hat from which a plait of material hung down toward her shoulders.

I soon realized that none of the other kids in the ward could see my night nurse and something told me her visits should remain a secret between the two of us. I was the only one she came to and this made me feel special.

I still remember vividly how she stood by my bed watching over me, always there when I woke in the night. Her gentle face looked like that of an angel. She gave me a feeling of total calm, the best medicine in the world.

She is the first spirit that I can recall in detail, though I'd seen vague shadows and had odd feelings from the age of three. I suppose that is why the arrival of my night nurse didn't trouble me; I was used to seeing figures that no one else did. I told no one about her visits simply because I didn't think they were out of the ordinary. It was just what happened. Not until I reached the age of eleven or twelve did I realize that my special night nurse had come from the spirit world.

So, what of the accident which put me in hospital? I had run home from my Essex village primary school excited and bursting to tell all about my day. A neighbour had called around to visit my mum and, chatting away, they both looked toward me as I ran into the room. But Mum had left a bucket of boiling water on the step between the living room and kitchen and I didn't see it until I ran right into it. The whole neighbourhood must have heard my scream. Never before or since have I experienced such agonising physical pain. Tears streamed down my face, great sobs shook my body making me gulp for breath.

Mum was beside herself and didn't know what to do. Tentatively, she removed my socks and as the skin peeled away with them I screamed even louder. Flesh exposed, my feet were red raw. I was taken in an ambulance straight to hospital, admitted to the children's ward and there I stayed for nine weeks – a long, long time to be away from home.

Sad and lonely, I would look down at my bandaged feet and wonder how long it would be before I could go out to play again, run around and kick a ball with my new school friends. I cried for my mum, even though the nurses were wonderfully kind to me. And my secret nurse was kindest of all. I smile now as I recall the comfort her visits brought – every night, after lights out, her words soothed better than any other medicine.

'Don't worry,' her soft voice would reassure, 'you will get better and the pain will go away soon.'

Having my night nurse with me was just like having my mum there.

It was not only painful feet but also asthma which kept me from sleep and I would often lie awake, crying quietly. Then I would look up and see my spirit nurse sitting by my side and she'd talk until I dozed off. While the other children slept I would watch her, transfixed, but when I opened my eyes in the morning she would have vanished.

Hospital visits from my family were few and far between. This was the late 1950s when long working hours and the distance they had to travel between home and the hospital made it difficult for them – in those days not everyone had their own car.

On one visit my Grandma Mercy brought me a toy

cowboy with some toffees hidden inside. I was over the moon. However, because some parents couldn't afford to buy sweets, the ward had a strict rule that any we might be given must be handed over so they could be shared equally by all of us. Being a typical boy, I didn't want to hand over my sweets and kept my stash a secret. Nothing got past my spirit nurse, of course:

'I know about your sweets in that toy,' she teased one night. 'But don't worry, Dennis, I won't tell anyone.'

I know of other psychics who, like me, experienced their first memorable spiritual encounter when they were sick. They, too, were sent guardian angels who offered help when it was most needed. I never knew the name of my spirit nurse, or why she picked me, but I will always be grateful for the relief she brought during that difficult time.

I was born on 15 July 1954 in the tiny, marshland village of Paglesham. Eight miles inland from Southend-on-Sea on the Essex east coast and bordered by two rivers, the Crouch and the Roach, the village has been renowned variously for ships, smuggling, fishing and oyster production. And with rough country tracks and paths right on the edge of its two hamlets, East End and Church End, Paglesham offered its children the pleasure of running free at play outdoors. We lived in a cottage in Church End.

My father, Jock McKenzie, hailed originally from the

village of Newtown St Boswells in the Scottish Borders, also home to our McKenzie clan. This is famous rugby country and Dad – well equipped with the big, strong McKenzie physique – used to play regularly in local games there. I inherited my father's build but have always much preferred football to rugby.

We lived in Paglesham, my mother's home town, until I was seven. While my father worked hard as a baker, my mother, May, had her hands full looking after four energetic kids. My brothers, Stuart and Murray, are older than me by six and four years respectively and my sister, Jacqueline, is four years my junior.

As a child I often felt lonely and left out by my siblings. I used to think this was because of our age differences but as I have come to grips with my 'gift' I wonder – though I didn't know it at the time – if it was because I was 'different'?

Strangely, I have no strong memories of my brothers and sister during our childhood years. In fact, I never felt very close to my immediate family, that bond just wasn't there. For example, I have no recollection of my eldest brother, Stuart, either as a child or even living in the cottage with us – though, obviously, he did. My memories of him begin to register only when he got married. I draw a blank on Murray, too, up until I went to secondary school. Why my memory of them should be like this I don't know. Perhaps a spirit decided to keep me cocooned while I was growing up so I would be ready to use my psychic ability, or it could just have been that being that bit older than me they weren't around much at the time. I do have vague childhood memories of Jacqueline – probably because she is younger than me – and I am also a little more in tune with her than I am with my brothers.

In common with most people, I remember virtually nothing prior to the age of three or so. Thereafter my memories are scant but vivid: I recall our dog getting distemper and dying when I was about three, hospitalization aged four and various relatives including grandparents and my mum's Uncle Stan – he'd lost a leg in a hay making machine and when he'd whip off his wooden replacement to show me I thought it was hilarious.

I did feel a bond with my grandfather on my mother's side, Golden Victor Cardy – what a wonderful name – who lived in the village's East End. He was, on the whole, a quiet man but could be very stern if you upset him. Grandfather was a natural countryman and wonderful with animals and from him I inherited a love of the wide open rural landscape. During school holidays I would often swap Church End for East End to stay with him and Grandma Mercy. There was a gravel pit on grandfather's land and I'd spend hours fishing it. It didn't matter that there was no money to buy me a rod, I made one out of bamboo cane which was good enough to sometimes hook a tasty trout for our dinner.

Grandma Mercy was a big tease, though she used to scare me, too – I could never tell when she was pulling my leg:

'I'm a witch,' she'd say, 'and I often fly over your house to see you, Dennis.'

I'd shudder, terrified yet enthralled. Did she really have such powers? She showed me her cauldron on the farm in Paglesham. I imagined her stirring up frogs and toads. Looking back, I think there was something psychic about her.

However, the person in our family who I was especially close to was Uncle Murray, my father's brother. He was the most charming of men and, true to the McKenzie genes, a big, thick-set guy. During a spell as a professional musician my uncle had fronted the Murray McKenzie Dance Band in his hometown, Newtown St Boswells. Before I was born, he and his wife, Shirley, had moved south to run a pub in the village of St Osyth, also on the Essex east coast. Over time, they became like adoptive parents to me.

The relationship between my uncle and me was particularly strong during my teenage years when I used to spend a lot of time with him at his pub. Uncle Murray was very protective toward me and I could talk to him about anything and everything. I was five when I first told my father about the spirits I'd seen but he'd have none of it; my mother, too, found the concept hard to fathom, though as I grew older she gradually became more receptive to the idea that I might have some kind of special talent. Uncle Murray was the only person who took me seriously and seemed to understand what I was talking about. I was devastated when my favourite uncle and confidant died as a result of alcoholism; ten years later, drink killed his wife, too.

I was about forty years old, and Murray had been dead for six years when his spirit started communicating with me – it was good to hear his Scottish twang again. One day, he communicated a very specific message: I was to ask my father about a bible which was in Canada and shouldn't be there and I should, also, describe to my father a special family watch and must refer to an occasion when my father walked across the bridge over the River Tweed. To me, the message made no sense at all but when I conveyed it to dad he knew exactly what it meant and was astonished at its accuracy. It turns out that in his family it had always been agreed that this bible would be given to my father, but that a cousin had stolen it before emigrating to Canada. There's no way I could have known about this story, it had never been mentioned before, so to see my father so amazed by what I told him made me feel that perhaps from then on he'd be a little less sceptical about my psychic abilities.

Uncle Murray had also mentioned something about me 'having the gypsy in me'. When I raised the subject with Dad, out came the big family secret. My late Grandma Jean, a Rutherford, had been a Scottish Romany gypsy but when she married outside gypsy blood, her people ostracized her. In addition, and sadly for Jean, the McKenzie family she had married into were ashamed of her gypsy roots.

'Maybe Grandma Jean is the reason you see your spirits, maybe you're like her,' Dad conceded.

I was speechless. Yet, of course, it made sense. My father's mother had the look and features of a Romany – dark, heavy-lidded eyes; dark, curly hair – and always wore lots of jewellery – bangles and lucky charms jangled on her wrists and she was never without a gold chain. Grandma Jean had always hated me and I, in fear of her, kept my distance. She must have sensed my psychic ability but rather than bring us together, it drove us apart. I reminded her of the life she had lost when she married my grandfather and for that she detested me.

When I was seven my father gave up the bakery business and became landlord of a pub called The Sun in Gold Street, Saffron Walden, near Cambridge. Once, Grandma Jean accused me of stealing a KitKat biscuit from the pub. It wasn't true but, naturally, my parents believed her word over mine and they were livid with me. At the time, I couldn't understand why Grandma had done this to me but now I know: she resented me for the gift I had inherited from her.

Our move to Saffron Waldon suited me well because my parents were so busy running the pub that I was left to my own devices. But I wasn't on my own for long because I soon found more friends than I could ever have hoped for – friends of all types and ages. My new friends, however, were not ordinary people but special, spirit friends – just as my night nurse had been – and they came to see me almost every day. The spirits didn't knock on the door or want to play football in the garden. They *flew* in to visit me. I would watch, gobsmacked, as they flew – not a broomstick in sight – around the pub's garden and landed on the sloping roof of an old shed. Incredible as it seemed I had no choice but to believe, to know, that this was really happening.

I was mad about DC Comics, American publications which featured characters such as Superman and Batman, and thus chose to pretend that my spirit friends were my personal superheroes.

'What shall we play today?' I'd ask them.

'We'll leave it up to you, Dennis,' they'd reply.

We talked and played hopscotch and running games and we'd spend hours together by the river, my friends sitting on the bank watching while I fished. When they took their leave I'd call out, 'See you tomorrow,' and be looking forward to the next day.

We always had great fun together and over the three or four years that my family lived at the pub, my friends' visits became part of my everyday life. Whenever I talked about these friends to my parents they just laughed and referred to them as my 'imaginary mates'.

All kids, my parents reasoned, have imaginary friends. For example, on a family outing to Dryburgh Abbey near St Boswells, while we were looking around near the Chapter House – once home to the abbey's monks – I suddenly saw a group of monks in brown cassocks. They didn't speak, but walked in file straight past me. I turned immediately to my mum, 'Did you see them, Mum?' I asked her. She turned to me and, without much urgency, said, 'What, Dennis? Have you been seeing your imaginary friends again?' I knew there was no point in trying to explain what had really happened.

At the pub in Saffron Waldon I also encountered my first nasty spirit, one who scared me. Every time I was sent down to the pub cellar to fetch drinks I would feel a chill sweep over my body and sense that something sinister was nearby, watching me. Then, when I'd peer over my shoulder into the cellar's dank gloom I would see a shadowy image. It was terrifying.

At the age of twelve or thirteen I watched a TV programme that helped me begin to make sense of my various spiritual encounters. The programme suggested that people who saw ghosts were actually seeing 'pictures caught in time' and described the spirit world as a 'residue of energy' which – for whatever reason and though there is, in reality, nothing there – some people can tune in to.

That explanation made sense: I was able to see a moment in time that had gone, there was, in fact, nothing there but nevertheless, residual energy remained that I could tune in to.

Most psychic people I have spoken to describe feeling, as I did, 'different' or 'special' as children. In my early teens, and in view of my parents' reaction to my 'imaginary friends', I elected to avoid ridicule by telling no one about my spirit friends. When I had first told them, my parents were so dismissive that I became wary about bringing up the subject in their company again. Like I said, Uncle Murray was an exception, I could always be open with him, and discuss things that I'd never dream of talking about with anyone else. While I was accustomed to seeing spirits wherever I went, including at school – in the corridors, walking around the playground – there was always something particularly weird about seeing them running along beside my living, breathing schoolmates.

My dad's pub business went bankrupt when I was ten and we moved to a village called Linton, in Cambridgeshire. I was by now at secondary school and being psychic enabled me to get what I wanted out of people. Because I could tell what they were thinking, I could wrap them around my little finger. I was, nevertheless, frequently caned for getting into fights and being disruptive.

When I wasn't at school, my happiest days would be

spent fishing – Linton is surrounded by unspoilt country-side and winding streams. Invariably, one or more of my spirit friends would join me on the river:

'Tight lines,' they would say.

'Yes, too true,' I would reply, grinning at my haul.

I had become an accomplished angler to the extent that the local doctor was prompted to request, via my mother, that I take fewer fish. He had the fishing rights on the river and I – though he had failed to catch me at it – had been poaching his trout. And they were delicious.

By the age of fifteen I was desperate to leave school. Studying was not for me and more than anything in the world I yearned for the outdoor life, to earn a crust from the countryside and work alongside animals. I felt my destiny was to be a game-keeper – I'd even got a job lined up but my mother refused to allow it, insisting it wasn't 'good enough for our son'.

I was deeply upset but had no choice. So I took a job as an apprentice electrician which bored the life out of me. I lasted about a year and then trained to become an appren-tice chef. I also worked on building sites, as a tyre fitter, in an envelope factory and as a pub bouncer. Job satisfaction? I found none.

Grandma Mercy died when I was eighteen years old. It was a desperately sad event for the whole family. On the night of the day she died, I was lying in bed thinking over all the good times we'd enjoyed when I suddenly sensed her presence close by and the room was filled with the wonderful, strong scent of lily of the valley – they were grandma's favourite flower and she grew swathes of them in her garden. Then I saw Grandma, sitting on my bed and looking every bit as real as when she was alive. She smiled at me and said, 'Don't worry, I'm fine.' And then she vanished. She had given me quite a shock.

I couldn't wait to tell Mum. By then she'd come around to the idea that I wasn't making all this kind of thing up. Mum found comfort in the words Grandma had spoken but Dad refused to accept what I'd seen and heard.

In fact, despite conceding that my psychic ability is probably inherited from his own mother, Dad persists in claiming that it's all a load of rubbish – but if anyone else says so, he's the first to jump to my defence.

I have two spirit guides: Jagna Anderson and White Cloud. Jagna is a German lady in her mid- to late-forties – quite young to have died. She looks typically Scandinavian with her short, blonde hair and she is attractive. I recognize her instantly when she appears in my mind's eye because she always wears very sharp, stylish business suits from the 1950s.

Jagna has been with me since I was seven – she was one of my friends in Saffron Walden. Over the years I've come to know her clear and unmistakable German accent so well – it's clipped and precise. And boy is she blunt in the way she talks and gives me information; it is she who I probably get my no-nonsense attitude from.

It was Jagna who helped me through secondary school in Linton. I'm the first to admit I was a bit of a school bully. Apart from sport I didn't like school one bit and would bunk off as often as I could but thanks to Jagna I always managed to pull off top marks in exams – her voice would whisper the answers to me.

We had a teacher called Mrs Tuller who was very, very big on speeches and presentations, and following a class trip to London to learn about William Shakespeare, we were to give an account of it in front of the whole school. I'd not been paying any attention, so when my turn came, I was totally unprepared. I froze. I stood up in front of 400 or 500 kids and wished the ground would open up.

Then, suddenly, the words flowed, fluent and articulate. Everyone stared, and then they clapped and clapped. Jagna had put the words into my mouth and saved the day, yet again. I shall never forget the wonderful feeling of coming top of the class for making that speech. Yet my mind had been elsewhere the whole time and I had no idea what I was saying. The teachers were amazed, and full of praise for my flawless performance.

My other guide, White Cloud, came into my life just before I became a professional psychic in the year 2000. He is an American Indian and one day I felt his spirit enter me and take me flying across the sky. We flew through big, puffy white clouds – so exhilarating – and so I named him White Cloud. I'd given him this name intuitively, yet it transpired that it was, already, my guide's name. He is with me for spiritual knowledge and healing.

He always shows himself to me as a very wizened old man wearing a breastplate and with a blanket decorated with triangles slung over his shoulder. When he shows himself to females, however, he appears as a young brave – probably trying to impress! White Cloud had sixteen wives.

A woman who came to me for some healing was fascinated when I told her about White Cloud and left determined to find out more about him. She tried a shop in Royston which sold memorabilia and mystic stuff. 'Sorry love,' she was told. 'Nothing on White Cloud, but we do have a pamphlet on White Eagle.' She gave me the pamphlet and a week later when I was lying on my bed reading it a very indignant White Cloud said:

'I am not White Eagle, I am White Cloud.'

No doubt about his identity, then. Soon after this, the same woman bought me a large poster depicting White Cloud exactly as I'd pictured him.

I used to hang the poster behind me at psychic fairs and one day, at a fair in Stevenage a fellow psychic saw it:

'The boss,' said the psychic.

'How do you know he is the boss?' I asked.

'That's White Cloud,' he replied. 'He's my guide and I call him the boss.'

It's not uncommon to share guides.

'I call him the boss too!' I said.

I married Janet when I was nineteen, after she became pregnant with our daughter, Donna. I wasn't earning much of a wage, so we began married life living with her family in their council house in Sawston, the largest village in Cambridgeshire.

I'd spent nights at that house before we married. Janet's parents allocated me the back box room but I had never liked sleeping there; as soon as I thought her mum and dad were asleep I'd sneak into Janet's bedroom. In the box room, sometimes, I'd seen flashing lights dancing all around the room at about pelmet height. I didn't know what to make of it. At first, I didn't say anything to Janet – we had only been going out together for a few months and I didn't want her to think I was weird – but it later transpired that she, too, had witnessed the lights. There's no way they could have been car lights because the bedroom looked over allotments.

While the lights were surreal, they were nothing compared to what I came face to face with one night in Janet's room. I am not the kind of guy who is easily spooked but that council house delivered the most spine tingling paranormal encounter of my life.

I woke with a start. 'What's that?' I yelled. An eerie, shadowy figure stood at the end of the bed. He wore a dark trench coat. He had a pointed nose and receding hair, swept back. I looked at it, at his evil face, and screamed. An icy chill in the room made my spine crawl. The sense of foreboding and dread was suffocating.

I screamed as loudly as I could and, with that, the spectre suddenly disappeared. My scream woke Janet who had somehow continued to sleep after I'd shouted out the first time. Shaking with fear and disbelief I struggled for words to describe the evil I'd just seen before me.

'Don't be so stupid. It's my Elvis Presley poster,' said Janet.

And then she went back to sleep.

But I knew that it was not Janet's Elvis Presley poster; rather, it was one of the most damaging and bad spirits I have encountered. Who he is and why he appeared remains a mystery.

On a more lighthearted note was the curious case of the disappearing underpants. Like most men, when I undress I throw my clothes on the floor and – unless someone else picks them up – there they stay until morning. Not so on the floor of Janet's room where my underpants would have vanished from where I'd left them the night before, and my wife certainly hadn't picked them up.

After nine months, Janet and I moved just around the corner

to a house of our own. A little while later, Janet's parents separated and her mother, Mavis, moved into Janet's old bedroom. She laid a new carpet and decorated it. Mavis had been using the room for a couple of months when my underpants started reappearing – dozens of pairs that had been missing for three years started turning up under her bed.

There must be some kind of vortex in that room that spirits – good and evil – use as a gateway in to the house. Despite that, and all that's happened there, Mavis still lives in the house, though she has moved back to her own bedroom.

Janet and I were excited to move into our own place. It was a council house, end of terrace and nothing posh, but we have since bought it and made it into a comfortable family home.

Having left one spooky house behind us, the last thing I expected was to inherit a spirit within our own four walls – but we did. At first she would do silly, mischievous things. For example, before we installed a shower we'd rinse our hair using a margarine tub to pour the water and the spirit would grab hold of the tub just as you'd be about to pour. 'Hey, let go, give it back,' I'd shout, but it didn't make a bit of difference.

Our resident ghost was playing games with us – everyone in the house has had some experience of her antics, sometimes reminiscent of scenes from the TV comedy *Bewitched!*.

Friends of our kids, Donna and Daniel, have sensed the ghost's presence, too. The kids' friends were always welcome, they knew they never had to knock on the front door, that they should just walk straight in. But that soon stopped when they became aware of our ghost. My family were used to hearing the ghost's footsteps walking around upstairs and it didn't bother us at all (except for the day when Daniel woke to find the ghost sitting at the foot of his bed) but it scared the wits out of the kids' friends.

Some fifteen years ago, on a night when Janet was out, I was asleep on one of the twin beds in my room. I opened my eyes and saw this woman – late thirties or early forties, short brown hair, quite slim – lying on the other bed, propped up on one elbow and looking at me. Our ghost. She wanted to talk but, 'Not tonight, I'm too tired,' I told her and, sadly, she has never attempted to speak to me since. This spirit has also sat on the bed next to our son, Daniel. Daniel regards himself as a brave, macho kind of a guy – he is a no-nonsense, high-rise steel erector now – but she scared the living daylights out of him and for the next week Daniel slept on his big sister Donna's bedroom floor.

When Janet went out for the evening I'd take myself off to bed and, often, I'd think she must have come home early because I would hear footsteps upstairs. I would call out to Janet then realise that it wasn't her but our resident, restless spirit. Sitting in the front room we'd hear her footsteps on the stairs, or she might rattle the letter box.

One day, a new yellow shirt of Janet's vanished. She'd liked it so much that she bought another one exactly the same. Then, three months later, the original one turned up on Daniel's bed, neatly folded on his pillow. Thinking about it makes the hairs on the back of my neck stand up. I'd love to know why our spirit wanted Janet's shirt.

I don't know her name or who she was, why or how she died, or why she wants to be in our house. She has never caused us any harm and she has never deliberately tried to frighten anyone so, we have just become accustomed to her being around. I have tried to talk to her but she doesn't want to get involved. She seems happy enough being with us, I just wish I knew who she was and why she can't let go of this house. We've lived here for thirty years now; I last heard her shuffling around upstairs some six months ago.

The string of meaningless jobs I'd done to pay the bills and provide for my wife and children had not diminished my love of the rural life and, at the age of thirty-eight, I decided it was time to pursue my dream. I became a gamekeeper and I had never been happier – out and about in the fresh air, no two days were the same and I never minded the long hours. I worked at Hinxton Hall near Cambridge for eight years and enjoyed every minute. I helped organize shoots and looked after thirteen dogs which I trained and bred from. I would never be without a dog but these days, since I'm away from home so much, I'm down to just three spaniels.

I had continued to see spirits every day and, as a general policy, kept these sightings to myself. As I reached the age of forty, my psychic feelings were becoming stronger and I also developed a tingling sensation and a heat in my hands which, I later discovered, is a sign of the ability to heal.

It was around then that I started to tell people other than my family about my psychic feelings. It was something that I'd bring up, tentatively at first, with some of my close friends. As time went on I began to be a lot more open about it. Gamekeepers don't earn a great deal and it was while I was moonlighting – a little door work – at the Queen's Head pub in Sawston, that I told a friend, Alex Willis, about the voices in my head and my hot hands. Alex didn't miss a beat, 'That's because you are healer,' he said. I laughed, nervously. I had no idea what he was talking about. It may seem odd me saying this now, but at that time the word 'healer' didn't really mean much to me at all. I asked him what he meant and he looked me straight in the eye and repeated, 'You are a healer.'

A few weeks later at a fellow keeper's party I was talking to his wife, Judith. We had met before and I knew we shared common ground about spiritual matters. Judith asked if I'd 'seen anything lately?'

'No,' I said. 'But this guy Alex reckons I'm a healer.'

'Okay then, Dennis, my back's killing me. Will you have a go at it?' asked Judith.

My hands burned so hot you could poach an egg on them. I did as Judith asked and placed my hands close to her back for about ten minutes. Twenty minutes later the pain in her back had gone. Not believing it possible that I could have cured her pain I convinced myself the result must be psychosomatic.

Meantime, we'd moved on to talk about the atmosphere I was picking up in the couple's home: something didn't feel right but I couldn't put my finger on it. Then Judith confessed she'd been having problems with a spirit. Though her husband wasn't bothered, it had rattled her so she asked if I could help; Judith knew there was something in the bedroom but couldn't say what.

Judith was right. In the bedroom I saw a petite, sweet-faced girl. She had long, straight, honey-brown hair and big eyes and was wearing a dress with a white bib over it which looked Edwardian. The girl told me that she'd drowned near the house where Judith lived when she was a child.

'That makes sense,' said Judith. 'I remember hearing that a girl had drowned there many years ago.'

'Well,' I said. 'She's attached herself to you for some reason and followed you here. She's quite harmless, poor little thing.'

Driving home that night I nearly jumped out of my skin when I saw that little girl sitting in the back of my car, smiling at me. It was bizarre but I didn't feel remotely scared or worried – in fact, I felt really calm. The girl wanted peace, and I think she found peace that evening. She sat in the car until we were close to my home and then disappeared. And she never returned to Judith's house again.

Judith's home became a calmer place but I was becoming increasingly confused. These spiritual experiences were powerful but I had no understanding of them. I took Judith's advice and made an appointment with a psychic, a woman called Phyllis Cole in Saffron Walden. One Friday morning at half past ten, I knocked on her door.

'What are you doing here?' she asked eyeing me up and down.

I told her I had an appointment. But that was not what she had meant:

'You don't need an appointment with me,' said Phyllis. 'You're the most powerful healer and psychic I've ever met.'

I laughed uneasily. I hadn't expected that. Why was this happening to me? Phyllis – in her sixties and smartly dressed – invited me in to her neat semi and then quizzed me:

'You see spirits, don't you?'

'I see something.'

'And you can hear them in your mind? They talk to you

in your mind, with girls' voices, and boys' voices and different accents.'

'Well, yes, but doesn't everyone?'

Phyllis told me firmly 'no', this was not something that happened to everyone, it was something special that was happening to me. Then she made a couple of predictions about how my life would turn out.

'You'll give up gamekeeping within a year. And your name will be known the world over.'

I just laughed at her. I had no intention of giving up the job I loved. A year later, however, her words rang true when my boss said:

'Sorry, Den, we can't afford the shoot any more. We're going to shut it down.'

The estate had held shoots for 120 years but, unbelievably, this was the end of an era and I'd been made redundant.

Phyllis had, somehow, opened the floodgates and since talking with her my connection with the spiritual world had been growing ever stronger. No longer confused and uncertain I was instead completely convinced I had found the right path to follow. I was forty-six years old and had decided I'd take the plunge and become a professional psychic. I believe the spirits decide when is the right time and for me that time was now.

* * *

Starting a new job is always a worrying time but Phyllis Cole had given me the confidence to take this path – indeed, she had predicted it.

I'll never forget the first reading I did. I was at Newmarket leisure centre and Liz, a woman in her mid-twenties, sat with me. She was incredulous when I told her she was pregnant, 'Absolutely no way. I'm not trying and I'm not pregnant,' she said. Liz contacted me two months later and told me she must have fallen pregnant a day or two before I gave her that reading. I can't describe how reassuring it was to get that feedback, it gave me faith in my ability.

When I first turned professional I asked White Cloud to 'give me just enough'. At that stage I was scared of being one of those psychics who is consumed by the ability, I wanted enough to simply make a living and help people while still living my normal life. I soon changed my mind.

White Cloud had given me exactly what I asked for but, eight weeks later, driving on Central Avenue in Newmarket I was sick of 'just enough'. I'd realized I couldn't dip in and out of this world, I must live and breathe it. It had to consume me. There was also the financial aspect of my business. 'Just enough' meant exactly that, there was no money left over once I'd paid the bills. Money has never been my motivation, but I must provide for my family and take responsibility for ensuring a reasonable quality of life that periodic bookings and occasional phone calls can't provide.

So I said to White Cloud, 'That's it, I've had enough. I want ample.'

'My son, you can have ample, but you will work for ample,' he told me.

And since that day my diary has been full. I have to work at it, but it's full.

I am sometimes asked whether I have had any training for this work. The answer is no. I strongly believe that if you have talent and ability, your spirit guides show you the path. My psychic ability is raw, natural and untrained. No one has ever helped me, except my spirit guides. My ability is something I shall continue using as long as I can, as long as the spirits want me to.

It's important to give back to the spirits, too. I will help anyone who has the ability. I can't teach them anything because it's already there but I can help them to recognize the ability they have and to hone it. I make no charge for such help, I see it as my way of giving something back to the spirits. We should never take them for granted.

Two years after turning professional I visited Soham following the murders of Holly Wells and Jessica Chapman – both just ten years old. After working there with the Wells family my life changed completely. In *Goodbye, Dearest Holly*, the book he wrote in memory of his daughter, Kevin Wells describes how greatly my ability impressed him and this has brought me international renown.

Inevitably, the way I work seems very strange to those who don't understand it. I can hear spirits – this is known as clairaudience; I can see spirits – clairvoyance and I can empathize and feel with spirits – clairsentience, which literally means 'clear feeling'. All this happens at the same time and then I interpret the information. The skill lies in making sense of all that information in conjunction with my instinctive feelings for the person I'm reading for.

I read for one guy, for example, whose maternal grandfather came through. I kept hearing the name Jim.

'He keeps saying Jim, his name is Jim,' I said.

'Yes, his name is Jim,' the grandson confirmed.

'He has got to be Irish because he keeps showing me green fields,' I continued.

Yes, the late Jim had been Irish but more to the point, his surname was Greenfield. Suddenly it all made sense and in that one sentence I had seen, felt and heard everything. Making the connections and linking together all the information is the most crucial element of my ability.

I usually start off a reading with numerology, which tells me about a person's character and what has gone on in their lives previously, what is happening currently and what is still to occur. White Cloud gave me the numerology method I use and it is, therefore, unique. My method is based on a person's name and date of birth and, sometimes, I include a street name, house number, married name, single name and even a nickname. Each letter and number gives me an accurate in-depth description about that person. From that, I move on – as a medium – to link the person to anyone they have a connection with in the spirit world. After this, I use tarot cards to look at their future.

I can do twenty readings a day, no problem at all, and not feel tired. Why should I be tired? I'm not using up lots of energy; it's the spirits that come through to me who are doing all the work. All I do is open my mouth and talk. Digging holes in the road is much harder work. The only time my work is hard is when it is a very emotionally charged and tragic reading.

Should you ever sit with a psychic who tells you they are always right – get up and walk away – we are fallible and sometimes spirits can get confused when they deliver a message: even spirits sometimes get their wires crossed. On the other hand, psychics can think they are wrong when they are, in fact, one hundred per cent right.

For example, I read for a lady three or four years ago and it seemed there was nothing in the reading for her – as nothing made sense to her. I apologised saying I was obviously way off the mark and wouldn't be charging but gave her the tape recording anyway. Later, she told her next-door neighbour some of the things I had said. Interested, the neighbour borrowed and listened to the entire tape and it turned out that absolutely everything on it was meant for her. She was so amazed that she insisted on sending me a cheque.

Just as I believe I inherited this ability from my Romany grandmother, I believe our daughter and son have inherited it from me. For now, neither of them is interested in using it as I do. Or maybe this is not yet the right time in their lives?

Donna certainly has psychic ability, as does her eight-year-old daughter, Sky Lucy. Daniel, too, has experiences with the spirit world. None of them has ever sought these encounters, they have happened just as they happened to me.

Donna Marie, our eldest child, is now thirty-four and married – she's an army wife – to Mark. Mark will soon be off for a tour of duty in Afghanistan and we shall all be worried sick about him. My ability doesn't help me find out what will happen to him, it doesn't work like that.

Donna and I have a unique bond. I can call her without opening my mouth – it used to annoy her. 'What do you want, Dad?' she would ask, before I had uttered even a syllable. She would often run in to a room, certain she had heard me calling for her. I hadn't called her, but she sensed I wanted her for something and she was always right. Notwithstanding, my daughter likes her privacy and doesn't go out of her way to tell people that I'm a psychic.

Donna has frequent clairvoyant experiences – she sees spirits sitting on her bed – and because she has learned from me about such experiences she's perfectly comfortable about it all and, as I mentioned, has no desire to develop her ability any further.

Sky, perhaps, will want to pursue her wonderful ability. Until she was aged two or three, she always called me Granddad. Then she suddenly started calling me Granny, which gave us all a good laugh, though it caught on and now all the grandchildren call me Granny which attracts some strange looks from passers by. When I asked Sky why she was now calling me Granny she pronounced:

'You know Granny, when my mummy and daddy weren't my mummy and daddy, you were still my granny.'

In a past life I must have been her grandmother and she has made that connection through her own spiritual ability. So, that's how Sky sees me.

Daniel is thirty-one and built like a true McKenzie. As it did with me, the ability seems to be growing in my son as he gets older. But Daniel is content with his life and work and, in the same way as his sister does, accepts his psychic ability as an integral part of his persona.

Last year, out of the blue, he announced that he thought he was getting 'a bit of this psychic stuff'. When I asked him what made him think so his reply blew me away:

'Well, I was in Cambridge one night in the car and I had

a phone call from a friend. He was telling me he'd got a new girlfriend. So, I asked him if she drove a blue Peugeot, and the guy said she did.

'Then I asked if she had blonde hair, and the guy said she did. And then I asked if she had got two kids, and the guy said she did. Then I gave him the registration of her car, of somebody I had never met before.

'Then I looked to my right and instinctively knew that the girl in the car parked next to me at the traffic lights was the girl this guy was talking about on the phone.'

This was something Daniel had worked out totally for himself which was fantastic – I was delighted. It's good to know that the ability is being passed on in the family. And when my time comes for the spirit world I'll still be able to chat away and moan at my kids and grandchildren – and have some fun with them . . .

There is no scientific reason for my ability or for why I have it. All I know is that, for the moment, I have it – it is with me. Is there something different in the psychic's brain? Many, many people have tried to find out what makes psychics psychic but one of the biggest obstacles to getting anywhere is that the minute the psychic opens up to scientific experiment, the ability stops working. Reads like an easy cop out? No, it's not, it's the spirits saying, 'We're not playing this game.' It is all on their terms and that is the way it should be.

Soham: the Painful Truth

'Thank you for your remarkable contributions during my darkest days.'

Goodbye, Dearest Holly, Kevin Wells

Holly Wells and Jessica Chapman were dead. My German guide, Jagna, had told me, and she is never wrong. Worldwide, millions of people would watch and wait, willing the safe return of those two innocent little girls – they were only ten years old. I wished desperately that Jagna could have given me some hopeful news but, instead, I had to tell Holly's parents, Kevin and Nicola Wells, the truth that would break their hearts.

On Sunday 4 August 2002 Holly and Jessica vanished suddenly and without trace. It had been a glorious day and Kevin and Nicola had made the most of the weather by hosting a barbecue for family and friends at their home – Kevin had been in his element cooking the meat and making sure everyone was having a good time.

A little before noon, Jessica had popped over to give Holly a necklace which she'd bought for her on holiday. The girls were excited to see each other again and swapped girlie news. Holly's close friend Natalie had slept over the night before and was collected by her mother around half past twelve. Natalie couldn't know as she smiled and waved goodbye, politely thanking Kevin and Nicola for letting her stay, that that would be the last time she would ever see her friend Holly.

Jessica stayed on at the Wellses' for the barbecue. The afternoon flew by – happy, summery, sociable – with family and friends sitting down to eat at half past five. The girls finished their meals and at around a quarter past six they could be heard in Holly's bedroom. When their guests were leaving toward twenty past eight, Kevin and Nicola called to the girls to come downstairs and say goodbye. There was no answer and after a quick look around failed to find them, the full-scale search began in earnest.

The day after the girls disappeared one of my clients, Leanne, phoned me – just after lunch on a warm, summer afternoon. I hadn't seen her for about a year and assumed she wanted to book a reading but I was wrong. She spoke quickly:

'Dennis, two girls have gone missing, will you please work on the case?' asked Leanne.

Leanne knew Kevin Wells's sister in-law, they were friends. I had given her a good reading in the past and her first thought had been to ask for my help. This was the first I'd heard of the missing girls but the urgency in her voice drove my response, I didn't hesitate for a second:

'Of course I will, where are they from?'

'Soham,' said Leanne. 'Can we meet today?'

I knew where Soham was – East Cambridgeshire, some twenty miles away and agreed to meet her. It would be vital to hold some personal items belonging to Holly so I could make a good connection with the spirit world:

'Can you bring something of Holly's along with you?' I asked.

Leanne understood, said she could arrange that and we agreed to meet at six that evening in a pub car park in Fordham, about one mile from Soham.

During the two years I had been working as a professional psychic I'd acquired plenty of regular clients and was pleased I could earn a living from my ability. I did not know on that summer afternoon in August that my life was about to change beyond all recognition.

I drove into the pub car park in Fordham feeling very apprehensive – with a sense of foreboding, and a heaviness inside me. Leanne was there when I pulled in. Her husband had been one of the many friends and neighbours out all night helping to search for the two girls. She said:

'These are sensible girls, Dennis, they just wouldn't go off on their own. Their families are mad with worry.'

Leanne had brought a few of Holly's personal belongings – some school work and items of clothing. I took them in my hands and, as I held them, I heard Jagna's voice, clipped and clear:

'They're dead.'

Blunt and precise as always, my spirit guide offered no more than to repeat:

'They're dead, Dennis.'

Jagna has never let me down and thus I have come to trust her word without question. There was no reason to doubt her now. Wretched and sick inside I felt immense sorrow for the little girls' families. Now, I had to be the one to tell Holly's parents – I didn't even know their Christian names. But I couldn't tell a third person – not even Leanne – my message from the spirit world. Would Holly's parents want to meet me? I couldn't force them to. Yet only I could convey Jagna's message; they had to hear it from me. When terrible information like that has come through you, I think it's your responsibility to deliver it personally. It may not be the easiest thing to do, but in my opinion, to leave it to a third party would be wrong. I turned to Leanne:

'There's a red vehicle involved in this, but I need to meet

the parents. I will get more if the parents are with me rather than you.'

Leanne looked anxious. She, too, was desperate to help and she must have been hoping for something positive from me, something that might reassure and help find the girls. She surely sensed my reluctance to tell her anything, but that was how it had to be.

'If Holly's mum and dad want to speak to me, I'm available,' I told Leanne. 'Just pick up the phone and I will be there.'

Later that night I heard from Leanne that Holly's parents would like to see me and I suggested we meet the following day, Tuesday. By now the hunt for the missing girls was national news and I watched the TV reports, feeling sick in the certain knowledge that both girls were dead. I agonised over how I might break my heavy secret to Holly's parents.

I did also offer my help to Jessica's parents, Leslie and Sharon Chapman, but they preferred to decline and I naturally respected that.

On 17 December 2003 Ian Huntley, a school caretaker at Soham Village College, was found guilty of murdering Holly Wells and Jessica Chapman. Huntley's girlfriend, Maxine Carr, who lived with him and worked as a learning support assistant at St Andrew's Primary School, was found guilty of conspiring to pervert the course of justice. Huntley had been employed as caretaker, a job which provided his tied cottage next to the school, for some nine months and had been known and trusted by many in the community, including Holly's father. Carr worked in the girls' class at St Andrew's Primary School and had been well liked by both children.

Kevin and Nicola Wells were, of course, incredibly busy dealing with the search for their daughter, the police and the press and therefore it was not until Wednesday 7 August that we first met. By the time we came face to face in Soham I was in turmoil. How could I do this nicely? I couldn't. When people come to me they deserve the truth, and nothing but the truth – even the kind of truth that will break a parent's heart.

Soham is just a thirty-five-minute drive from my home but I had never had cause to visit the town before that day. It was an easy journey, along the A11 on a stretch of dual carriageway normally bumper to bumper with commuter traffic, but that day the road was quiet – August, school summer holidays. Off the slip road onto the A142 and I was soon in Fordham from where Soham was only minutes away.

A thriving rural town proud of its agricultural heritage and good schools, Soham boasts a tight-knit local community – many families having lived there for generations – where people have always felt safe, where their children will come to no harm. The Fenland town was now rapidly, sadly, gaining notoriety.

I stopped off briefly in Fordham to collect a talented psychic, Lorraine, for whom I have great respect. I wanted to take her with me to see if she would pick up the same message as I had from the spirit world. Lorraine had taken an interest in the similarly high profile case of Sarah Payne, the eight-year-old abducted and murdered by Roy Whiting in 2000. My mood was very subdued as we drove the last mile to Soham. As soon as we hit the main road into town we saw large numbers of police cars and, everywhere, police talking to people and taking notes. Hundreds of volunteers had joined to help the police and both girls' families in the search for Holly and Jessica.

We drove one hundred yards or so along the main street – I noticed Soham Village College, the town's secondary school, ahead – then turned right into Tanners Lane – passing a group of Victorian terraced houses on our left – then right into Red House Gardens, the cul-de-sac where the Wellses lived.

The modern properties, mainly detached houses, in the cul-de-sac sport neat front gardens. The family had moved there about a year ago and Holly (and her friend Jessica) went to St Andrew's Primary School while her brother, Oliver, then aged twelve, attended nearby Soham Village College – both within a short walk of home. Kevin runs a contract cleaning business, Nicola is a legal secretary with a local firm and both have worked hard to provide for their home and the family they love.

Lorraine and I were standing on the street when Kevin and Nicola walked toward us. Kevin's bald head was distinctive anyway but I recognized both parents from the newspaper and TV coverage. Nicola's sunken eyes, rimmed by dark shadows were swollen from the tears she had shed.

Kevin Wells was gaining widespread admiration for the courageous way he was handling himself under the media spotlight and, while Nicola was much shyer than her husband, I, too, admired the couple's quiet dignity and self-control.

The normally quiet cul-de-sac was packed with friends and neighbours who had rallied to help in any way they could. As Holly's parents approached us the crowd stared at Lorraine and I. Did they know who I was or why I was there? I introduced Lorraine and we followed Kevin and Nicola into a terraced house across the road. This was not the Wellses' house, but I did not know that at the time. I felt wretched knowing I was about to shatter all hope that they might find their daughter alive.

Kevin and I shook hands. I was feeling very awkward, but wanting to offer some comfort I hugged them both. Once inside, I did what I always do in order to feel more in tune with the spirit world: I looked for some space on the floor and then lay down on my tummy and stretched out. Understandably, Kevin and Nicola looked on in amazement but this is what works best for me – except, sometimes, I lie on my front on the sofa. It looks eccentric, and maybe more so because I'm a big bloke, but I don't care because I know that's how it works for me.

I heard Jagna's voice again, repeating the same terrible words she had said before. 'They're dead, Dennis.' Lying on the floor, nervous and anxious, I asked myself again how I should deliver Jagna's devastating message. I felt a gnawing in my stomach, I wanted to be sick and my mouth dried at the thought of what I must tell. How would I feel if someone said, 'Dennis, Donna Marie is dead'? I thought about that and felt the pain. Or what if it were my grand-children? But this wasn't about me, this was my work. Would I compromise? Would I lie?

Holly's parents were sitting close together on the sofa, holding hands. Nicola looked as white as a sheet. I looked up from the floor and asked:

'How do you want this? Do you want me to be blunt and honest?'

I waited for their answer but I knew it didn't matter because I can only be blunt and honest. They looked at each other but they didn't speak, then Kevin said:

'I don't think this is any time for pussyfooting around, we want you to be as honest as you possibly can, we want to hear the truth, however dreadful.'

Then I told them, straight:

'I am really sorry, but both the girls are dead.'

Jesus, it was like a bomb, it was as if I had just lit a two-second fuse. I was looking at Nicola and I could see her face kind of frozen in time – it was like a mask came over it. Then silent tears started trickling down her cheeks, slowly at first then faster and faster until they streamed. Kevin appeared nonplussed. I understand, now, that Kevin is a master at hiding his emotions.

It was a moment charged with incredible emotion and I sobbed with Nicola at the overwhelming blow my message had dealt and because their pain was palpable. I had never, ever had to say anything so terrible to anyone. Words cannot describe my feelings.

'Are you sure?' Kevin asked.

I nodded. Nicola's silent tears fell more heavily. Kevin wanted to know more and asked:

'Are you talking to Holly then?'

'No, Kevin, I am not talking to Holly. I am talking to my guide, Jagna, and she is telling me that she is dead, that the girls were dead before half past seven on Sunday evening.' Still lying on the floor, I described the vivid pictures that were now coming into my head. There were two people, a woman and a man. The woman was a shrew-like creature with features to match and brownish hair. The man was in his thirties and had short, dark hair. He also had a swagger about him and was not an intelligent man.

Neither of these two people was local to the area. I also described their accents as 'Northern'. I'm not very good on accents and, by 2002, I'd only been out of Cambridgeshire on a handful of occasions. I couldn't have told you if an accent was from Hull or York or Manchester, I just knew it was Northern – that is what my spirit guides were telling me.

It became apparent after their arrests that these descriptions matched Maxine Carr and Ian Huntley respectively who both came originally from Humberside.

There was more. I could see the car – an old, red, Ford Fiesta – which had been used to transport the girls' bodies out of Soham: Huntley drove a red Ford Fiesta. I carried on saying things as they came to me.

'The girls were wrapped in something, possibly bubble wrap, but likely carpet. The girls have been moved away from Soham.' Then I described a scene present in my mind's eye. I felt I was looking out of a window of the house where Holly and Jessica had been murdered. I continued:

'There is water next to their house and it is a straight piece of water like a ditch. There is a very tall building, possibly a windmill, but without sails in the background. Ducks figure prominently on this piece of water.' I later learned that this ditch runs close to the tied cottage next to Soham Village College where Huntley and Carr lived, and that the ditch ran to a huge, conical grain silo nearby – looking at it in the distance, I had mistakenly identified the grain silo as a windmill with no sails. I kept hearing a song, 'Prickwillow, Prickwillow, Prickwillow'. Kevin put two and two together and told me there was a windmill at Prickwillow, a small village I had never heard of near Ely.

All this would be relevant to the location where the bodies were found ten days later:

'Go down a straight track and there is a ditch to the right,' I said. That's the scene I kept seeing in my head which I felt was significant.

Kevin and Nicola sat holding hands tightly while I continued to describe what my guides were telling and showing me. I felt the letter J was of significance, I could see a road with grass on both sides which I believed the girls had been driven along and also the number 18. The letters C and O were very prominent in my mind and formed part of an address of a property – I could see it was an address which Kevin had walked past while searching for Holly. All this eventually made sense. The letter J and number 18 featured in the registration number of a van belonging to Scott Day, Kevin's business partner and both men had been driving around in it searching for Holly. They had stopped outside the school where the van would have been visible from the window of Huntley's cottage. It was that which brought it into my mind's eye. And the letters C and O? Part of Huntley's address in College Close on the edge of Soham Village College.

Meanwhile, Lorraine had picked up the same shattering message from her own spirit guides.

'I agree with Dennis, both the girls are dead,' she said. 'I'm so very sorry, but that's what I am picking up, too.'

To have to hear the grim message repeated must have been very hard to bear. Lorraine then left us and I wasn't sure what to do next until Kevin asked if I'd visit some houses with him, properties where he had his suspicions about the inhabitants. He was curious whether I might come up with anything. I desperately wanted to help and agreed:

'Yes, of course, Kevin, that's no problem at all. You've got me for as long as you need me.'

We stepped out into bright sunshine under a clear blue sky. Kevin was still keeping his emotions under wraps. Nicola went to speak to an elderly lady – a relative I think – and seemed to be telling her what I'd said because they were crying. As I walked down the front driveway, I could feel the crowd's eyes boring through me. I had the heaviest of hearts.

Kevin crossed the road to what I later realized was his home, then came back and said:

'Right, I'll drive us into town and then we'll walk to these houses.'

He had a list of twenty-five addresses he wanted to check out including three where he reckoned the occupants were particularly shady. He didn't tell me which three but, interestingly, I honed in on the same ones – nothing to do with the murders however, none of the addresses brought us any clues.

I sat in this bereaved father's car wondering if telling Kevin and Nicola about Holly's fate had been the right thing to do. And I came to the conclusion that, yes, I can only tell the truth as I see it, it's my job to be truthful. I, also, wanted to convince Kevin that I was credible and, for that reason, told him some very personal details about one of his friends I had met at the house at dinnertime.

That day I saw what a good actor Kevin could be: he seemed very composed on the surface, so together, so cool. He had just found out that his beautiful daughter was dead yet there was no anger. I so admired his strength and courage. I sensed that he needed to be practical and busy all the time, doing anything which might help find his beloved daughter and her friend, Jessica. Not one to sit around waiting for the phone to ring, his first priority was to check out these addresses.

Soham High Street was a couple of minutes' drive from Kevin's house. As well as the heavy police presence there were lots of media reporters and cameras about – the place had been invaded by outsiders – but the street remained busy with shoppers, people going about their business and kids larking about. Everywhere you looked there were 'Missing' posters showing Holly and Jessica, wearing identical Manchester United shirts and smiling.

Kevin parked the car and we walked along the high street. Most of the locals obviously knew Kevin – he'd probably cleaned their windows – yet they were avoiding him. He may not have noticed, but people were crossing the road when they saw him coming, not making eye contact. It doesn't mean to say they weren't out there helping to search for the girls, they were just struggling to find any words they might say to the parents. Convinced that Kevin must be feeling raw and vulnerable, I really felt for him.

In fact, more than 500 local people turned up to help look for Holly and Jessica on the first day of the police search throughout Soham and its surrounding villages. The girls' parents couldn't have wished for more loyal support. Fen people are doers rather than talkers and, at the end of the day, that's what counts.

Suddenly, Kevin's face lit up. He'd spotted a man in his early thirties, and what was great was that this guy came right over and spoke to Kevin:

'Anything else I can do, mate? You know we're all here for you. We'll do whatever we can to help. How's it going? Is there any new information?'

'No, mate, nothing new,' Kevin replied. And then he introduced me:

'This is Dennis McKenzie, he's a top – well, what would you call yourself, Dennis? I think you would say he's a psychic guy.'

'Well, if you need any help, you know where I am,' said Kevin's friend – words that must have been much appreciated.

We stopped off at five or six of the properties on Kevin's list. Some were houses that had been converted into flats now used by itinerant land workers; the area was a magnet for them because of the opportunities for work.

I stopped suddenly at one door and put my hand on it. I felt heat surging through from the energies surrounding it and knew there was something amiss. I said:

'This is nothing to do with the girls, but there's something here. I think it's to do with drugs.' It later transpired that a drug dealer was living there.

We went to another house but we couldn't get near it as it was surrounded by other people – I sensed a chilling, vigilante mood. As for the woman who lived there, I said to Kevin straight off:

'She's nothing to do with it.'

Because I was with Kevin, I think I must have looked like some sort of official. For example, we met up with the police at a block of flats above some shops and when Kevin told them we were going to walk around they said:

'Yes, if that's what you want to do. Do you need to get into any of them?'

Kevin passed the question to me, and I said:

'No, we don't need to get in. If I get a feeling, we just need the police to go in afterwards.' We continued walking along the street. In fact, we were within 800 or 900 yards of the killer's house and we would have got to it if we had taken a right turning off the high street. If only we had taken that turning I would, I'm sure, have picked up a spiritual connection which could have provided some significant leads. But we didn't. We walked by a car salesroom opposite a pub called The Ship alongside which I was drawn to a low wall, like one you might find in a garden. I stopped dead in my tracks. I'd sensed an important connection. I turned to Kevin:

'There's something about right where we are, here.'

He looked at me closely and asked what I meant.

'There's just something about this spot, it's connected to a phone or a phone call.'

I pointed toward a nearby ditch:

'I feel that ditch is connected, somehow. I wonder if a phone has been dumped in it?'

Kevin said nothing, he just looked at me.

I later learned that this ditch runs along the back of Huntley's house and is the one that runs to the grain silo at Prickwillow.

Three months later he told me:

'You know that wall where you stopped me? I remember coming out of The Ship some twenty years ago and sitting on that wall with two girls. One of the girls was Nic [Nicola] and the other was a close friend. That was the first time I'd met Nic and our relationship blossomed from then – that's why you felt that spot.'

'No, mate,' I told him. 'That's not why I felt something at that spot. I stopped because I felt something with a phone, not because it's where you met Nic. Some psychics might be saying to you now, "Yep, that's it. I picked up that energy," but the reason I stopped was to do with a phone.'

During the murder trial it transpired that Huntley had phoned the friend who'd been with Nicola on that night in The Ship the evening before he murdered the girls to ask her out for a date. I knew it was something to do with a phone.

When the two school friends left the Wellses' family barbecue at around a quarter past six on the evening of Sunday 4 August 2002 Jessica Chapman had her mobile phone with her. Some two hours later Holly's parents realized Holly and Jessica were not in the house and they, and the Chapmans, began trying to track them down – it was totally out of character for either girl to go off for any length of time without parental consent. Mrs Chapman tried calling Jessica's mobile but it appeared to be switched off. The girls were reported missing to the police at a quarter to ten that evening.

They were last seen alive at a nearby sports centre where they went to buy sweets at around half past six.

Kevin and I kept on walking and came to a bridge:

'I feel that Jessica's phone was thrown into the river here,' I told Kevin. He looked incredulous. Repeated searches have failed to recover the phone, yet I feel very strongly that this is where it ended up.

Next, I described in more detail a scene in my mind that I'd touched on during my reading in the morning:

'I want to go somewhere where there's a road with grass on either side, where you might see sheep or cattle. It's like a little road running through a common or something.'

Kevin recognized it: we turned into Paddock Street and walked one hundred yards or so past a mix of quaint Fen cottages and contemporary houses to an area of open grassland divided by the road – exactly as I'd pictured it. I marvelled at the perfect match: my clairvoyance had shown it as clearly as if I'd seen it on TV.

We were standing by a wildflower meadow. Cattle grazed here once and though there are none around today the cattle grid's still there. These days, mature trees stand amid grass grown tall; archetypal England. I imagined Holly and her friends cycling over here, picking the buttercups – grinning and holding them under their chins to test if they liked butter or not. East Fen Common – and I sensed it straight away – was important:

'This is it, Kevin. The girls left Soham on this road.'

'This road leads to Prickwillow,' said Kevin.

I began to sweat profusely – my shirt was soaked, sweat poured down my face. It was a hot day but this was melt-down. The colour drained from my face and I felt sick. My eyes became cloudy and translucent, my pupils dilated. When I make a strong spiritual connection the full force of the energy surges through my body rendering me help-less in the vice-like grip of paranormal power. Kevin looked on, aghast.

Prickwillow was just seven miles away – turn left at the end of East Fen Common and you're there. Everything was pointing to Prickwillow. Kevin phoned a woman he knew who lived in a windmill there:

'We need to get to Prickwillow. We need to look at this piece of water that leads to this windmill.'

I stood by while Kevin called his police liaison officer to let him know that he was going to go with his friends to follow up this new piece of information.

Despite this potential lead, Kevin remained emotionless and poker-faced. With his arrangements now in place he turned to me and said:

'Well, Dennis, thanks for your help, thanks for what you've done.'

'You know where I am if you need me,' I told him.

He took out his wallet and asked how much he owed

me. He didn't owe me anything, I never dreamed of charging a penny.

'You've been out here helping me. I've got to pay you.'

'No,' I said. 'You don't pay me for telling you your daughter's dead.'

Before he left for Prickwillow we shook hands and he thanked me for my help. I knew deep in my heart that those little girls had been murdered, yet my parting words to him were:

'Kevin, I have never been wrong when I've said someone is dead. I hope and pray that I have got it wrong on this occasion.'

Everything I'd told Kevin that day, he passed on to the police. They never asked to speak to me but I don't blame them – I know they are inundated with calls from psychics in cases such as this one. There are gifted psychics who might help a case but there are also, sadly, charlatans and time-wasters and it is, in general, impossible for the police to know who might offer genuine help.

Driving home from Soham, I wished I could have picked up more messages which might unearth the perpetrator of these vile murders. I still couldn't forget the chill in Jagna's voice when she had told me about their deaths. For the sake of the parents, I would do whatever I could to help find whoever killed those girls.

Back home, I switched on the TV and two bright, beautiful faces smiled at me: Holly and Jessica in a photograph taken just before they sat down for dinner with Holly's family, little more than an hour before they went missing. Holly had wanted a picture of herself and Jessica wearing their new Manchester United football shirts. Both girls were huge Man United fans and idolized David Beckham. Two pretty ten-year-olds without a care in the world, best friends showing off their new, identical shirts for the camera. The newsreader was broadcasting an appeal for information about their disappearance. I knew they could never be found alive.

When I first met Kevin Wells in the flesh I'd been struck by how closely Holly's face resembled his. She had, apparently, been a real daddy's girl and the apple of his eye. Nicola described the daughter she will always miss as her soul mate. Blonde haired, blue eyed Holly had been a typical English rose. Her short life was filled with a whole variety of interests from cooking and writing poetry to dressing up in girly frills. She'd marched with the Fenlander Majorettes – wearing her smart costume with pride and twirling her baton high – and had loved being a bridesmaid for various friends and relatives. What's more, Holly and her dad would join up and give their karaoke version of Robbie Williams's 'Angels' at one of the local pubs.

Over the ensuing few days the blanket media coverage

concerning the girls' disappearance continued. I sobbed and sobbed. I had never before – or since – been affected so deeply by anything in the course of my work as I had by the Soham murders. I couldn't stop thinking about the pain their families were suffering. I wondered, too, if Kevin and Nicola had told Jessica's parents that I believed their daughters were dead.

When Holly and Jessica slipped out of the house to go and buy some sweets, they didn't tell anyone they were going out and no one heard them leave. They were seen by passers by – arms linked, wearing their red shirts – walking a foot-path that would take them past Ian Huntley's home, the modern, detached house which he shared with his girlfriend, Maxine Carr. Carr was not at home that evening. She was one hundred miles away in Grimsby, visiting her family.

Minutes before he spotted the girls on the footpath, Huntley had slammed down the phone on his lover after a furious argument in which he accused her of cheating on him. When he saw the girls walking by it is thought he suggested they come and say 'hello' to Maxine, thus luring them inside the house.

Ian Huntley was the last person to see Holly and Jessica alive.

Police, family and other volunteers continued to search for

the missing youngsters. Kevin, of course, had been combing the area day and night. After we first met in Soham, he rang with the news that two girls had been seen in Little Thetford, a village eight or nine miles from Soham. I knew it was a false alarm and told him so:

'Forget it, Kevin. You're dealing with a lunatic. This is someone who wants their fifteen minutes of fame. The girls are not walking anywhere.'

'Okay,' he replied quietly. I think he was shocked at how forthright I'd been.

The report, from a woman who said she had seen the girls 'larking about' in Little Thetford, was soon discounted as unreliable by the police.

A few days later, on the twelfth of August, Leanne phoned to tell me that the girls' bodies had been found. For obvious reasons, I was curious to know the location.

'They've been found just outside Newmarket, on the heath,' said Leanne.

I knew instantly they were not the girls' bodies and said so.

Nothing had been reported in the media about this when Leanne spoke to me, she had heard about it from Kevin. She told me that two mounds of earth had been found, the area had been cordoned off and the families had been told by police that they believed these might be shallow graves and connected with the disappearance of Holly and Jessica.

I knew this had to be wrong. This site didn't match the one I'd envisaged. I was adamant:

'I don't care what you've been told, Leanne, the bodies are not buried outside Newmarket. Tell Kevin and Nicola it's not the girls.'

Next day I learned that the 'graves' at Warren Hill Gallops had turned out to be no more than an innocent badger's sett. How can anyone confuse a badger's sett with a human shallow grave? As always, I felt for the families.

While it remained on my mind and I continued to follow the media coverage, that was my last direct involvement with the case until two weeks later when I went to visit my friend Ruth who was having a brain shunt operation in Addenbrooke's Hospital, Cambridge. Ruth, who lives in Fordham, is also friendly with Leanne – both women had been part of a group I used to read for in that area. I was glad we had kept in contact, I like it when clients let me know how they are getting on.

Ruth knew I had been in touch with the Wellses and, while I sat by her bed, she asked for my thoughts on the Soham case and what I thought had happened to the girls. As I was telling her what I had told Kevin, a new picture came into my head:

'I can see a long piece of water and it's like the piece of water as you drive up from Five Lamps roundabout, as if you're going to Brandon fourteen miles north of Soham.

It's like a piece of river, but slow running. There's a bridge and a straight piece of water, and I keep seeing that piece of water. I don't know why.

'I can also see a bungalow and there is a caravan in front of it and the drive is on the left of the bungalow. For some reason, Ruth, I think this bungalow has connections with the case.'

I didn't mention any of this to Kevin because we hadn't spoken for a while. I don't feel it's my place to go invading people's space, telling them things they may not want to know. I'll always wait until I'm asked, and I know that at the time I was just one of the different leads Kevin was following up in his attempt to find Holly; so our lack of close contact was hardly unusual.

On 17 August 2002 Huntley and Carr were arrested at the home of Huntley's father in Littleport, some thirteen miles from Brandon. As soon as I saw the report on TV I recognized the bungalow – with a caravan in front of it and a drive on the left. After the bodies were found I learned that the 'piece of river' was near Lakenheath, just inside the Suffolk border. This rural location is home to the largest US Air Force-operated base in England. On the same day that Huntley and Carr were arrested, a walker discovered the little girls' bodies in a remote, overgrown irrigation ditch alongside a rough track and close to the perimeter fence of Lakenheath airbase

– some fifteen miles north of Soham. The route the jury were driven to visit the site took them through Prickwillow.

When I'd read for Kevin that first time I'd been straight with him and explained that I hadn't been able to speak to Holly on the other side. Usually people are disappointed if I can't make that connection. With Kevin I felt that, even in the smallest of ways this had somehow kept a tiny flicker of hope alive. As it turned out, it wouldn't be long before Holly did make contact with me. She came through to me of her own accord; in fact I didn't initially even know who she was. However, as she relayed the information I was later to pass on to Kevin and Nicola, it soon became heart-breakingly clear.

A few days after I first met Kevin and Nicola I'd noticed a missed call on my mobile. I didn't recognize the number but called and got through to Kevin:

'I just wondered if you have got any more information or thoughts, Dennis?'

'The girls are definitely dead, Kevin,' I told him.

'What do you mean?'

'Well, I spoke to Holly.' I'd delivered the words with my customary bluntness. There was silence on the other end of the line as I relayed to them the details of my conversation with Holly, complete silence. After I read for Kevin and Nicola on Wednesday, I was certain they had grasped the fact that the girls were dead:

'The girls are definitely dead, Kevin,' I'd said; now it was this sentence that extinguished Kevin's last hopes that she was still alive: 'Holly is lying face down somewhere, almost as if she is floating. It is not in deep water though, I really am sorry.' He hung up very quickly. We had spoken for no more than a few seconds.

When I talked to Kevin on the phone that Friday I had failed to recognize that he and Nicola still held out a vestige of hope that the girls might be alive. This time, however, my message had hit home. I was oblivious to this at the time, and it was not until three years later when Kevin sent me a copy of *Goodbye, Dearest Holly* that I realized the terrible blow I had unwittingly delivered.

In his book, Kevin says he was still hoping, still cherishing a dream that Holly could be found alive. He describes how, when I returned his call and told him – again – that his daughter was dead, that the words 'just snuffed out that one tiny flicker of light at the end of the longest of tunnels'. When I read that, I cried for the pain I'd inflicted.

As soon as he'd hung up the phone Kevin burst into floods of tears: his heart was tearing up. Nicola wanted to know what was wrong and he told her he'd been speaking to me. She took one look at Kevin and knew what I'd said. Holly was dead. Hope was dead.

In the copy of *Goodbye, Dearest Holly* Kevin sent me he had inscribed, '*Thank you for your remarkable contributions during my darkest days.*' The words moved me greatly. I needed to speak to Kevin – to apologize:

'I've rung because I want to say I'm sorry, mate.'

'What are you sorry for? You've got no need to say sorry to me,' he assured me.

'I've just read a little bit of your book. The inscription is lovely.'

'It's meant from the heart, Dennis.'

I went on to say that I didn't realize when I called him on the phone that he and Nicola were still hoping Holly was alive.

'Of course we were clinging to hope,' said Kevin. 'Just because you said she was dead and you said you hadn't got her talking, we thought maybe she was still alive. Until you kinda knocked that last hope out with that sentence.'

'I'm so sorry I was that blunt. I didn't realize how you would take it,' I repeated.

Then I cried like a baby. Kevin cried, too. Then he said something wonderful – wonderful because it meant he appreciated the help I'd willingly given and knew I'd delivered my message straight, as he'd asked me to:

'Don't you cry to me, you fat bastard. You helped us and I wanted it delivered that way.'

*   *   *

On August 16 2002, using keys found in Huntley's house, police unlocked and searched a storage building at Soham Village College. Here, hidden in rubbish sacks, they found the girls' trainers plus charred remnants of their clothing. In the early hours of Saturday 17 August police arrested Ian Huntley and Maxine Carr: Huntley on suspicion of murder and abduction of Holly Wells and Jessica Chapman; Carr on suspicion of murder of both girls. Later the same day, news that the bodies of Holly and Jessica had been discovered precipitated widespread mourning.

Huntley had set fire to the bodies in order to destroy forensic evidence and by the time they were found, both corpses were severely decomposed. Post mortems on both bodies were inconclusive but asphyxiation was deemed the 'likely cause' of death.

From the moment he was arrested there was never a doubt in my mind that Huntley was the killer and when the girls' bodies were discovered, the visions I had had made sense: 'Go down a straight track and there is a ditch to the right,' I had said and, even before Huntley was caught, Kevin rang to tell me that he, too, recognized the similarity.

On 21 August 2002 Huntley was charged with the murders of Holly Wells and Jessica Chapman while Carr was charged with attempting to pervert the course of justice by giving false information to police officers involved in a criminal investigation and two counts of assisting an offender. Huntley was sectioned and taken to Rampton psychiatric hospital, Carr was put on remand in Holloway prison. The trial at the Old Bailey opened on 3 November 2003 and ended on 17 December 2003 when Huntley was found guilty of murdering both girls and Carr guilty of conspiring to pervert the course of justice but cleared on two counts of assisting an offender.

The abduction and murder of two little girls brought Soham unwanted notoriety. But residents engendered a more lasting legacy for their town when they showed the wider world the true meaning of community spirit: unquestioning, immediate help for a neighbour. Within hours of hearing that Holly and Jessica were dead hundreds of grief-stricken well-wishers were placing flowers and pictures of the girls at Soham's St Andrew's parish church – within a week the outside of the building was covered in a mass of tributes and the path around the church was flanked by a wall of flowers numbering perhaps 10,000 bouquets from across the globe. The Wellses and the Chapmans invited more than 2,000 local residents plus friends, members of the girls' primary school and a number of police detectives to celebrate their daughters' lives in a service at Ely Cathedral at the end of August, this was the final public ceremony of remembrance. Jessica was cremated on 2 September and a day later Holly was buried, both at private funeral services, both held at St Andrew's parish church.

Soham may long be associated with the word murder but Holly and Jessica will always be remembered with the most tender affection.

Following our first meeting in August 2002 I did not see Kevin and Nicola again for seven months. Not wishing to intrude I'd decided to leave it to them to make contact if they wished and, so, I was delighted when out of the blue Kevin invited me over to dinner at their home. The murder investigation was underway but no information was filtering through to the family – he and Nicola wondered if I might shed any light on proceedings. They had come to a point where, without the regular contact with the police that they'd had before, their information as to what had really happened to their beloved daughter had dried up. Remembering the accuracy with which I had predicted so many things already, Kevin was hoping I might be able to tell them more. He promised me a 'nice steak meal' and I accepted with pleasure, more than willing to use my psychic ability to help in any way possible.

Police inquiries since Huntley's arrest had revealed that Grimsby's police and social work departments knew of him. During the time he lived there, before moving to

Soham, he had been investigated on four separate occasions for having sex with underage girls but there was never enough evidence to take things further; there had also been three allegations of rape and one of indecent assault and he had also been charged with burglary.

Only Huntley's burglary charge – which had been dropped when it came to court – was registered on the police national computer. No one in Soham had a clue about any of this. The police vetting in Cambridgeshire and Humberside when he had applied, having changed his name to Ian Nixon, for the caretaker's job at Soham Village College revealed nothing untoward. Huntley's cunning was such that he remained unsuspected within the local community. Even after he had killed Holly and Jessica he at first succeeded in persuading the police of his innocence, even helping an officer in her search around Soham Village College grounds in the early hours of Monday 5 August as well as when they questioned him and searched his cottage.

It was bitterly cold on the evening I drove to dinner with Kevin and Nicola in March 2003. While looking forward to seeing the couple again I also felt slightly apprehensive. I hadn't been in the town since the day I met the Wells family but I knew from media reports that Soham, though trying to move on, was still reeling from the murders.

When I pulled up in Red House Gardens I couldn't figure

out which house belonged to the Wellses so I went to the one where I had given my reading and asked for directions.

'Come on in, Dennis,' Kevin grinned. 'I've got a nice bit of steak to cook for you.'

What a lovely home they had. Everything was immaculate, as neat as a pin, just as I imagined it would be – Kevin and Nicola had always looked smart and tidy when I'd seen them on TV, despite their ordeal. The house mirrored their decorum – everything sat neatly in its place.

'How long are you here for?' Kevin asked.

'Well, you've got me for the night. I've cleared the diary for you.'

'That's great,' said Kevin. 'It's good to see you again.'

They called Oliver in and we were introduced. We shook hands, man to man. He was a real gentleman, just like his dad. Blond haired, too: he and Holly looked like two peas in a pod. Next, I told them I had been in direct contact with Holly in the spirit world:

'I have made contact with Holly many times over the past few months,' I said softly, and as gently as I could. I wanted Kevin and Nicola to feel at ease, and I knew that this would be a big thing for them to digest. As a way of making them feel more comfortable with what we were about to be entering in to I suggested that before I embarked on the reading I would begin with some numerology.

'Let me do your numbers to start with,' I suggested, and got on with it for all three of them. I've always felt that doing people's numbers is a good bridge between the every day and the other side. However, you have to draw the line somewhere and I have a rule that doesn't allow anyone to sit in on readings unless they are more than sixteen years old because it could prove disturbing for them. Many adults find it hard enough to grasp messages from the spirit world. Twelve-year-old Oliver was fine about it and arranged to go and visit one of his friends. I thought what a great credit he was to his parents.

Kevin and Nicola were genuinely interested in my work, so I explained the healing, regression and hypnosis I practise and hypnotized Nicola – just to show her what it felt like.

One way I connect with the spirit world is by making an energy ball. I began turning my hands around in circles as if smoothing them over a sphere – I could feel it growing. I continued, intense heat burning in my hands, encouraging the ball to grow to the size of a football. Then I thrust the ball toward Kevin and he was shot backward and fell, rammed by the power of supernatural energy. He had no idea what had happened. He picked himself up off the floor and, dazed, asked:

'Who pushed me? Did you, Nic? Tell me. Did Dennis push me?'

'No, Kev, no one pushed you,' answered Nicola.

She looked flabbergasted – they both did.

Because of the intense energy I create when I work with spirits the surrounding temperature changes rapidly to either freezing cold or boiling hot. On this occasion the air inside became so unbearably hot that my hosts had to take off their sweaters and switch off the central heating.

Kevin was still trying to work out who, or what, had thrust him backward with such force – he always needed to have an answer to everything. The effect of the energy ball served as further proof of my psychic ability, and with the paranormal, I explained, you learn to accept that some things just happen.

'I have to go outside and cool down,' said Kevin.

Nicola and I joined him, also glad to take advantage of the night's frosty air.

Holly's birthday was in February and, around the time she would have celebrated turning eleven, her family had put together a selection of more than a hundred photographs depicting their happy little girl at school and at play. Arranged on a Welsh dresser the images presented a joyful showcase of family life. Back inside the house, I looked at the pictures with interest.

Manchester United featured large, of course – the entire Wells household are rock-solid supporters. There was a picture of Oliver with David Beckham taken when, after

Holly's death, the family were invited by Cambridgeshire police together with Man United football club to be the team's guests of honour at a match. Beckham made public appeals for the girls to return home. He had also sent flowers to their funerals. Team manager Sir Alex Ferguson, with his squad lined up behind him had made a televised appeal for information. There, too, is the famous, final picture ever taken of Holly and Jessica – their Manchester United football shirts both had Beckham's number 7 on the back. And, unmissable among the photographs is a football signed by the Red Devils on the day the family went to see them.

'I can't have her last school photo in there,' said Nicola.

And me, being dumb, didn't click why that might have been.

'Because,' said Nicola, 'that bitch is in it.' She didn't raise her voice but the bitter hatred of its tone expressed more than words ever could – the cold pain in a mother who has lost a child.

I kicked myself. Of course, Maxine Carr would have been in the photograph. When Carr left the school at the end of the summer term – her temporary contract had not been renewed – soft-hearted Holly had made her a special card and bought her a box of chocolates.

We made small talk over dinner – steak and chips, cooked to perfection by Kevin – and then it was time to do what

I'd come for. Kevin and Nicola looked at each other nervously as I assumed my favoured position on the floor.

Within an instant Holly's spirit came straight through to me and I repeated her first words to her parents:

'Hi, Mum, hi, Dad.'

Then:

'I don't half miss shopping at Next on a Saturday morning, Mum.' Nicola laughed but, still, it brought a tear to her eye. She missed those shopping trips, too. When Kevin was playing his beloved cricket matches, mother and daughter would go shopping; Holly's favourite shop was Next.

Holly then spoke about a necklace and I said:

'Nicola, Holly would like you to wear that necklace of hers, which she was wearing when she was murdered. She knows it's a rubbish necklace but would really, really like you to wear it when you can.' Nicola was pondering which necklace this might be as I continued:

'It's a cheap necklace, but she's making me write the word love, not making me feel it or say it, but write love.' Nicola looked at me in disbelief. 'That necklace is with the police at the moment. They are trying to clean it up.'

Holly wanted to speak to her dad. She said she had seen him sitting on her bed, crying, and that this had made her really sad. She spoke about her cuddly toy, Snoozums, and said she'd seen her dad cuddling the toy and crying. Then she said:

'Tell Olls Holls loves him.'

Kevin and Nicola smiled. The children's nicknames for each other, of course: Olls and Holls. When I was speaking to Kevin later he told me how amazed they'd been that I'd picked up on this since it was an unusual pair of nicknames that only Holly and Oliver used. Then, Holly talked about the murder. Contrary to what Ian Huntley would later say during his trial, she said she was killed second and that Jessica was killed first. Holly went on to say that she felt no pain now and she didn't want to talk about it. It's often the case that murder victims don't want to say much about how they died. They don't see that as important. I could see that Huntley had his foot on the throat of one of the girls and knew that no blood would be found in the house although there was a cut to Holly's top lip during strangulation. To give that kind of detail was harrowing, really harrowing, and I felt immense sadness for Kevin and Nicola. Tears flowed down their cheeks as they listened, frozen at the horrors I was describing.

Holly started to talk about her best friend. I was bemused having assumed that this was Jessica but, apparently, Jessica was quite a new friend, a school friend. Holly wanted her love passed on to her best friend – Nicola, of course, knew who she meant.

Then Holly said:

'Tell Dad I was that seagull.'

It was an emotional moment. Far from Kevin showing the expressionless mask he had presented to the world at large, his true feelings shone through: Holly's words brought forth a poignant mix of sadness and joy. Very recently, he had read Richard Bach's classic *Jonathan Livingston Seagull*. It tells of an independently minded bird who determines to be more than ordinary; the skill and joy the gull attains as he strives to fly ever higher and farther are a metaphor for freedom and transcendence in death.

The morning after reading the book, Kevin had seen a seagull perched on the roof of the house. He thought it curious when the gull then flew down onto the road, and more curious still when he found a seagull feather tucked under the windscreen wiper of his van. Holly's words, therefore, were touchingly significant for him. In *Goodbye, Dearest Holly*, Kevin writes that after reading Bach's novella he had been able to go to bed that night with 'an inner sense of harmony for my daughter' for the first time since her death. Holly had seen this from the spirit world and wanted to send her dad a sign. The gull feather Kevin found on his van is very precious to him and has a special place on the Welsh dresser alongside the photographs and other reminders of the couple's little girl.

A white feather from a bird means an angel is looking

over you whilst you're alive, it is the most comforting and loving message that can come from the spirit world. It is not unusual for a spirit to appear reincarnated as a bird, though this was the first time I'd known one appear as a seagull; past reincarnations I have known have been in the form of a robin or blackbird – I have also known spirits appear as a butterfly. Overwhelmed by this information, Kevin couldn't hold back the tears.

Holly was worried about her parents:

'Tell them I've been standing by their bed watching them and I don't want them to be sad. I want them to remember the good times.'

That evening I also conveyed to Kevin and Nicola two dates which flashed before me, telling them one would be the turning point of the murder inquiry and the other would relate to money. I didn't know which month or year, only the dates. The first was the 29th and the second was the 9th. As I predicted, Huntley confessed to the murders on the first date, and the couple did receive money – a donation I believe – on the second.

Naturally, Kevin and Nicola asked me to pass on their love to Holly in the spirit world. And, just to make sure she heard they shouted, too:

'We love you, Holly.'

In contrast to the first time we'd met, that evening with

the Wellses was one of sheer joy. It was wonderful to be able to connect her with her parents and convey her words. There was great sadness that Holly was in the spirit world, of course, but the absolute, heartrending joy when I put Kevin and Nicola in touch with their daughter made me realize why I do my job. Words cannot express how much it meant to me that Kevin and Nicola understood that Holly had not gone. Their daughter was in a different place but she was still watching, she was still around.

That evening in March brought much comfort not only to Holly's parents but also to me. When we first met in August 2002 I had had no choice but to tell Kevin and Nicola that their daughter was dead. Jagna had told me and, therefore, I knew it must be true. Then as events unfolded I suffered as I read how my well-meant words were reported by the media: how could I have the gall to tell Holly's parents that their daughter was dead? Who did I think I was? I was heartless. I was aghast and pained that these reporters could present me in such terms.

That anyone could imagine I would, out of sheer malice, tell a parent their child was dead? To me, it was beyond belief and it hurt me very deeply. Did they not know I have kids and grandkids of my own? Yet Kevin and Nicola understood my motive was only ever to help. I wish those who have spoken ill of me would ask Holly's parents for their thoughts about what I did for them because that, surely, is what matters.

There is a strong bond between Kevin and me, forged in mutual admiration. I admire the way he has coped since his daughter's murder and how he has moved on with his life; he, on the other hand, admires what I did for him and his family at that time of crisis. Curiously, although Nicola is more overtly emotional than her husband, the bond between us is not as deep.

Kevin has been criticized for writing and making money from *Goodbye, Dearest Holly*. I, however, will always treasure my copy and understand that to write about his daughter was his own form of catharsis – his way of dealing with losing her and all that happened in the aftermath of her disappearance. He had made notes every day of everything that took place and everything that was said to him.

Over and above that, Kevin has donated proceeds from his book to two charities: Grief Encounter, UK, of which he is a patron, and Child Victims of Crime. Grief Encounter offers support tailored to the needs of each individual member of a bereaved family and was of great help to the Wellses after Holly died. Child Victims of Crime, the national police children's charity, helps children whose lives have been affected by crime in the UK.

Kevin is very modest about the work he does for them but those who work with him and those he has helped certainly appreciate his tireless support. He is prepared to give time and to revisit his own painful experiences in order to help others, and there is no doubt in my mind that that man deserves an honour from the Queen.

The trial at the Old Bailey in London of Ian Huntley and Maxine Carr did not begin until 3 November 2003 and two days later the prosecution opened its case alleging that Huntley had killed both girls at his home. More than fourteen months had passed since Huntley and Carr had been arrested but, now, the story was back in the headlines.

During the five-week trial the court heard Huntley's claim that Holly had drowned when he knocked her, accidentally, into the bath while trying to help her control a nosebleed. He claimed, too, that he had accidentally suffocated Jessica in the course of trying to stop her screaming. Manslaughter, then, not murder was one option the jury must consider. Originally, Carr claimed to have been in the house on the night of 4 August 2002 but later admitted she'd been covering up for Huntley. Carr's barrister had suggested that, like so many others, his client had been deceived by Huntley and had 'suffered enough'.

On 17 December 2003 after almost seventeen hours of deliberations the jury returned an eleven to one majority decision finding Huntley guilty of the murder of both Holly Wells and Jessica Chapman and Carr guilty of conspiring with Huntley to pervert the course of justice. Huntley was sentenced to two terms of life imprisonment – he will remain locked up until at least 2042 – Carr to three and a half years.

The jury deliberated for three days during which time I'd called Kevin and told him, correctly as it turned out, what I predicted the verdicts would be. I also predicted, also correctly, that Carr would not be spending much longer in prison. By the time she was sentenced Carr had already spent sixteen months on remand and was released on licence after serving a further five months.

I next met up with Kevin and Nicola at their home and with the trial behind them their mood was much lighter. 'Well, Dennis,' said Kevin, 'you were spot on with so many of your predictions. It really was amazing.'

They had asked me to give them another reading. Holly's spirit came through and I saw her lovely, smiling face. She spoke of a day toward the end of the trial when her dad had become very, very angry. Kevin explained that Huntley had left the dock and walked straight toward him and stood just two or three feet from him. There in the courtroom at that moment, Kevin felt a surge of hatred and wanted to kill him.

Then I saw Holly dressed in her majorette outfit, throwing her baton and looking pleased with herself. She had mastered a tricky twirl that had eluded her on this earth's plane: it was a lovely message to pass on.

There was still a lot of media interest in the murder story

and that month a special edition of *Tonight* was to be made and presented by Trevor McDonald, and would broadcast interviews with the parents. Kevin asked me if I would take part because he felt it was important for people to know about my work and my involvement with him. I was both touched and honoured by the faith he obviously had in my work so I was only too happy to be involved.

I then described how I kept hearing the Christmas carol *The Holly and the Ivy*. I asked:

'Have you got any idea what that could mean? It's more like I know Holly is *with* Ivy.'

Holly was named after the carol, explained her parents, and Ivy was Kevin's grandmother who has passed over. The chances are that Holly and her great-grandmother have been reunited, a thought that brought Kevin and Nicola further comfort.

I next spoke to Kevin when he called to say he was writing his book. He was including a lot about me in it and wanted to know if I minded, which I didn't. I trusted him to write with honesty and he had always made notes of our meetings so his information would be accurate.

When he sent me a copy of *Goodbye, Dearest Holly* when it was published in 2005 it made me feel so humble. I had really done so little while Kevin and Nicola were going through appalling torment. I was choked up by the kind words he wrote. Words such as:

'Dennis does indeed possess an extraordinary gift.'

'Thank you for your remarkable contributions during my darkest days.'

'I remember telling Nicola that I felt Dennis was a very talented medium. Here now in black and white is startling proof that he is the genuine article. It is a clear, first-hand indication that there is something "on the other side".'

'Little did we know the impact Dennis was going to have on our lives.'

Kevin told me that the book was going to be serialized in the *Mail on Sunday*. I had no concept of the impact that might have on my life until around nine o'clock one Sunday morning – the day that the first instalment of their serialization ran. I hadn't seen the papers yet so I had no idea how big a deal the book, and my part in it, had become. When I opened the front door of my house – intending to nip outside to fetch my diary from my car – I was confronted by some thirty reporters and photographers. I had no idea why they were there and here I was wearing just my boxers and T shirt. It was certainly a version of 'shock, horror'.

'Please don't take a photograph of me dressed like this,' I pleaded, and I'm thankful they didn't. I beat a hasty retreat into the house and said to the family:

'Oh my God, go and look outside.'

As soon as I picked up the paper from the kitchen table

where it had been lying unread and saw the headlines I realized the *Mail on Sunday* had chosen extracts which featured the story I had told the Wellses of Holly's death and the messages she had sent from the spirit world. Reporters camped outside my house for two days, knocking on my door and asking for my side of the story. To be honest I think they were trying to scupper Kevin's book's chances, and after all the kindness and gratitude he'd shown me, that wasn't something I was willing to go along with. My answer was the same every time:

'If you want to know what I have done, you will have to speak to Kevin or Nicola Wells. I'm not saying anything.'

It would not have been right for me to speak about the Wells family and I was certainly not going to break any confidences between us. Kevin's book would soon be in the public domain and he, of course, had every right to tell his story. The media continued to hound me for information – my phone never stopped ringing. I even had a call from the *News of the World* offering me a life-changing amount of money to tell them my own account of those dark days. Nothing could have induced me to talk to the media. I was, as I have said, convinced that it would have been a betrayal of the Wellses' trust so near in time to the tragic loss of their daughter.

I, however, had become known as the 'Soham psychic' whenever I was mentioned on TV or in newspapers. This was after the trial; I think it was the interest people had in Kevin's book that sparked it off. I became very embarrassed by it but, the name having been coined, I understand now that it's something to be proud of, even as the events surrounding Holly's murder recede into the past.

Notwithstanding, Holly's spirit still appears in readings that I give to people from Soham other than her parents. I see her pretty face – smiling. If someone sits in my house and I pick up Holly's spirit, it always turns out that they knew her. The first time it happened, I looked at the woman I was reading for and said:

'What's Holly got to do with you? I've got Holly here.'

She laughed and told me that she was a friend of Nicola's and that she had known Holly very well. So, I still speak to Holly occasionally.

When Ian Huntley and Maxine Carr were on remand awaiting trial I was working in Finchley and a young woman sat down opposite me for a reading. Straight away Holly's spirit came through and told me she knew her. I said:

'I've got Holly and she's showing me Soham and the war memorial in Soham.'

The woman smiled and said:

'You're the guy they call the Soham psychic, aren't you?'

'Yes.'

'I'm Maxine Carr's wardress,' she said.

This hit me like a bombshell and I asked the woman's

opinion of Carr but she turned the question around to me and I didn't hesitate to answer:

'I think she's a devious lying shit bag.'

Carr's warden looked me in the eye and said:

'You've got her in one.'

'I have to accept that I am in the presence of a most extraordinary man'

Goodbye, Dearest Holly, Kevin Wells

Being Psychic:
Life in the Third Dimension

I have been tuned in to the spirit world for as long as I can remember – since the encounter with my special night nurse at the age of four. Fifty years have gone by since then, during which time I have learned to come to terms with my psychic ability and, now, I know no other way of life.

Being psychic means living as if a TV is permanently switched on inside my head. All the time, I hear, see and feel the spirits who pass on messages for the clients I read for. Sometimes the signals I pick up are brilliant and I have a perfect image in my mind; at other times there is a lot of interference and the picture is fuzzy.

The spirits become particularly active at night and have a preference for dark, quiet rooms. I have learned that the only way to shut them up so I can get some sleep is to keep a bright light – or sometimes the TV – on in the bedroom.

A bedside lamp is too dim so, every night, the overhead light must be on or dozens of spirits could make their presence felt and I would have no peace. If I switch off the light, the spirits will become lively.

I not only hear them chatting away in my head, sometimes talking over each other as people might do in real life, but also see them walking around the bedroom. There might be two or three of them at any time and they appear as whole figures, as real as you would be if you were standing before me – not the shadowy, transparent ghostly figures which most people imagine spirits look like.

The spirits come through to me because they want to maintain some contact with humans and they're pleased to find someone here that they can communicate with. Like anyone else, I want to get a good night's sleep, yet if the spirits are lively I might catch just four or five hours and then I'm shattered the next day. I know other psychics who suffer the same problem and, we all agree, it can be a bloody nuisance. In the end, when my nocturnal visitors are really driving me up the wall, I just tell them to 'bugger off' and that usually works.

On a busy night there might be a dozen spirits chatting away in my head – some quite loudly, others faintly murmuring. When their voices are no more than a whisper, too quiet to hear what they are saying, it's rather like hearing but not listening to a radio playing in the background.

Of course, while I'm accustomed to living with various spirits chatting away inside my head, it can sometimes be a terrible burden. One spirit in particular, an old lady called Lucy, plagued me terribly. For months and months Lucy's troubled spirit kept coming through and wouldn't let me sleep. Over and over again, she would repeat:

'It will be my time soon, my time soon.'

I hadn't the foggiest idea what she was talking about and, finally, I said to White Cloud:

'You've got to stop this, it is driving me bloody crazy, it is absolutely driving me crazy.'

Lucy went quiet and, boy, it was wonderful to have some peace again. However, one month later, Lucy's spirit was back with the words:

'My turn this week.'

I was intrigued to know what was bothering her. Then, later that week at a psychic fair in Hertfordshire, an elderly lady came and sat with me and I was flabbergasted when, straight away, Lucy's familiar voice came through. 'This is it,' I thought. 'After Lucy's big build up I'm going to have the most astounding messages to give to this lady.' 'Lucy's here,' I told the client but she didn't seem very surprised, and just said, 'Oh, is she?' and explained that Lucy was a friend who had passed over. Then Lucy told me her message:

'Tell her I'm fine. I'm okay and my legs are better.'

Then she left. That was it. That woman had plagued me

for four months just because she wanted to tell her friend that her legs were better – albeit it mattered to Lucy and her friend. One question I cannot answer is, how did Lucy know four months in advance that her friend would be sitting with me? How do spirits know such things?

While the voices in my head occasionally weigh me down, ninety-eight per cent of the time I feel happy and placid. I am naturally easy-going and being psychic is, for me, normal. Very occasionally all the problems I hear in the course of my work get on top of me and I feel almost suicidal, as if I'm drowning in them, but I soon snap back out of it.

Anxious that I might let people down, I felt most under pressure when I first turned professional. Everyone who sits with me wants absolute clarification of whatever is on their mind. They expect miracles. They expect me to be able to tell them everything about their life and, of course, I can't. To know everything is impossible. In the early days I absorbed too much misery and unhappiness from other people's problems and suffered for it. But those dark days are now few and far between and tend to last no more than twenty-four hours. As a matter of self-preservation I have disciplined myself not to dwell on the tragedies I may hear from those I read for.

There is, of course, a lighter side to my work, too. One's personality in life is carried through into the spirit world and this is partly manifest in the way a spirit looks when it appears. For example, if a person was vain and liked dark hair but had grey hair when they died, they will show themselves with dark hair. Equally, when several voices are jabbering in my head it is perfectly clear which ones were bossy and domineering in life.

A reading I gave recently in Ireland shows how identifiable, and how amusing, such personality traits can be. The woman I read for had lost both parents. Usually, if they are partners, then both spirits will make their presence felt to their relative at the same time, but that didn't happen at this reading. The woman's father's voice came through first and from his soft tone I deduced he was a very quiet, gentle man.

'This is odd.' I said. 'I feel your mum's spirit, but she's not standing beside your dad.'

The woman then said she would have expected her mother to be first to come through at which, quick as a flash, her father came out with:

'Huh, and do you think I would have got a word in edgeways then? That's why I'm here first.'

One of the things people always want to know is whether people still sound the same when they've passed over to the other side. I think they're always a bit surprised by my answer, and I admit, it doesn't sound entirely logical.

When a spirit communicates with me the voice retains whatever tone and accent it had when it belonged to the living person. So, if the spirit had been a Geordie on the earth plane, they'd speak to me in a Newcastle accent.

If a person spoke no English at all when they were alive on the earth plane, they will speak to me from the spirit world in absolutely clear, precise English delivered in an accent even the queen wouldn't be ashamed of. In fact, if when I connect with them a spirit starts speaking absolutely perfect English with a cut glass accent I can tell immediately they're foreign. If I was to hazard a guess I'd say it was the spirits making sure that the messages they had to deliver got through without being misunderstood at any stage. Though matters can get a bit complicated if they spoke broken English when they were on the earth plane, because that's also how they'll communicate with me from the spirit world. I don't know why they do this, since it must surely be clearer to wait for this mysterious translation to occur. Maybe they're too impatient to deliver their message? Although those spirits who spoke a foreign language come through to me in English, this can sometimes slip, most often at the end of our session. It's almost as if once they've said what they really needed to they can relax a bit and let down their guard. On one occasion I was reading for a woman in Aberdeen and her father spoke to me in English, though with such a plummy accent I knew it wasn't his native tongue. At the end of the reading he came out with two sentences which I repeated as he said them though I didn't understand what the words meant. His daughter said:

'I didn't realize you spoke German.'

And when I said I couldn't she told me I had said to her, 'Goodbye, I love you my dear,' in that language.

Be it a happy or a sad day, at the end of each one I always thank my guides, Jagna and White Cloud, for what they have given me and for helping me. I thank them in my own way – they know me well enough to know how blunt I am. There is too much tendency among psychics to be reverential toward their guides. This is misplaced, our guides are here to, literally, guide; they are here for us. So, when I want something, I *tell* Jagna or White Cloud that I want it, but I know from experience that I must not be disrespectful. Five years ago, for example, I was angry about work and told White Cloud:

'That's it, I've had enough. I'm not doing the work any more. I'm sick of being there for everyone else all the time. When am I going to get something back from you in return?'

White Cloud's wise, wrinkled face looked like thunder:

'I've got ten more to fill your moccasins, my son.'

It was his way of giving me a big slap – just as an employer might tick off a member of staff. I realized I had been very disrespectful but, because I acknowledged the fact, three weeks later my life took a big turn for the better and I could see White Cloud's hand in it – very fair of him I thought.

In the course of my work, telling the truth is of the utmost importance. During a reading when I tell a client something they don't want to hear – such as a personal fault, or that their Mr Wonderful is trouble waiting to happen – they more often than not conclude that I must have been speaking a load of crap. Happily, six months later when whatever it was has come to fruition, those doubters normally return to number among my biggest converts.

There are others who misunderstand what I can offer them. For example, I read for a woman at my home one day and, half an hour after she left, she rang to say she was not happy with the reading. While she confirmed she was satisfied about the reading's accuracy she said:

'I'm meant to be feeling over-the-moon. You're meant to make me feel good and over-the-moon.'

I explained that my job is rooted in honesty – telling the truth as it appears to me. I'd told this lady straight what I felt her life was going to be like and she obviously didn't like it, but I can't help that.

The truth and straight talking are paramount when it comes to fiscal matters – an aspect of my work I regard as extremely important – and as a direct result of readings I have given, a number of people have reaped financial gain. Today, almost everyone is worried what effect the current global recession will have on them. Fewer jobs are safe and more and more people are asking me to read for advice relating to their financial security. Commonly, people will ask for a reading when their business is at a turning point or when they are wondering whether or when to start up a business.

It is very satisfying to help a business grow because of the benefits this generally has for employees. Few things in life are scarier than losing your job and your income – as I know from experience.

Working with businessmen such as James, from Nottinghamshire, is a great pleasure. We met after I read for his wife, Mary, who was so impressed by the messages I passed on from her father's spirit that she egged on her husband to see me, too. I read for him in person once or twice a year and he calls from time to time to talk through any troublesome strategic decisions.

When we first met, Jagna told me that important business decisions were uppermost in James's mind and I passed on her words:

'James, I can see that there is going to be a very strong business connection coming from the US and that you will be critical to it.'

Later, when James's employer completed a trading

arrangement with an American company, I saw this was the moment for change and that he should take a lead:

'Jagna is telling me that this is a good opportunity for you to start your own business, James. You've got to go for it now.'

Naturally, he wanted to know more and I was able to convey that the American company needed UK representation and that James should take on this role. Jagna was telling me that his commercial situation looked sound and strong and that he would be successful. On the strength of this, James and Mary started their own company in March 2005 – it has gone from strength to strength.

James will ask for psychic advice at times such as when he was going to the US not long after the company started to close a deal on which the company's success depended. I was able to give the reassurance he needed; in fact, I told him:

'You will exceed your expectations. You will come back with something more than you had planned for.'

I was also able to convey to James very precise information concerning the companies he was going to meet on which he would need to focus. He phoned on his return, ecstatic that he'd not only clinched the deal he'd gone to make but also landed a new contract with another company. Everything I'd suggested he prepare had, he confirmed, been exactly what he'd needed. I was delighted to hear such good news and it seemed that just as Jagna had helped me with my school work, so she, through me, was helping James.

Over the years, James, Mary and I have become friends and recently he mentioned a problem with a member of staff who was lacking commitment. Again, Jagna told me what action James should take – this employee should leave, she said. That was really tough for James but he went through with Jagna's advice and the person he fired is happier where they are now and James recruited someone more suited to the job in hand.

James has told me how interesting and beneficial he finds my advice – you won't find it mentioned in any business manuals, though.

I also work with two dealers who buy and sell on the stock exchange on the basis of recommendations from the third dimension. I connect to the spirit world and, again, it's Jagna who passes me the information. They are obviously doing okay – the fact they keep calling suggests Jagna's tips must be working in their favour. Then there was a lady from Greenford, a London suburb. She must have been at least eighty and she sat for a reading. I'm a big flirt and we were having a laugh and a joke. She was really good fun and we were having a nice time and then her father's spirit came through:

'He's reading a paper, but it's not a newspaper, it's like a horse racing paper,' I said.

She knew instantly that it would be the *Racing Post* or something similar and said: 'Well, ask him what's going to win the big race on Saturday.'

'Chris King,' came her father's reply.

At home that Saturday my wife Janet took a phone call from the old lady. 'How much did your husband win?' she asked. I am not a betting man so, of course, Janet didn't know what she was talking about, but the lady explained and said to tell me I'd been 'spot on'. The name of the winning horse had been Chris Kin, close enough when she saw it in the running order for her to lay a bet and win £460. It was wonderful to hear that the old lady's father had picked her a winner.

While I rarely bet on anything I was, once, tempted when I found myself in a casino in Aberdeen. I had been doing readings in the city until late at night and the casino was the only place still serving food. The tinkle and clatter of coins pouring out of the slot machines did not tempt me but my eyes were drawn to a girl playing roulette. I went over to her, then pointed out a number which I felt was going to be very lucky. She placed her chips on the number I'd indicated, then the wheel spun around and the ball stopped – to her obvious surprise and great delight – on her number. She went home £2,000 richer.

The girl's win tempted me to place a bet but Lady Luck wasn't on my side that night and I lost £500 in two minutes.

That's the spirits' way of telling me to lay off, that using my psychic ability to gamble is useless, it will not predict any winners for me. It's a reminder that I have my ability in order to serve others and it cannot be used for personal financial gain. On the subject of gambling, the lottery is one thing that all the psychics I've ever spoken to cannot use their paranormal ability to predict for themselves.

Our spirit guides do not provide us with all the answers to everything. Psychics, like everyone else on earth, must live and learn – learn from our experience of the world and its people and learn, too, from our mistakes.

For me, living with psychic ability has also meant giving up drinking alcohol. To ensure the best possible connection with the spirit world I never drank before giving a reading, but after a very embarrassing incident four years ago I gave up the booze altogether.

Away from home on a trip, I'd spent a night drinking heavily and next morning was nursing a whopping hangover. I was in a restaurant, trying to force down some breakfast when, suddenly, I felt a sharp, searing pain in my back. I gulped hard as I felt my insides lurch toward my chest wall. A sense of helpless panic gripped as what felt like a silk mask covered my face, its sticky film adhering firmly to my skin. Tentatively, I touched my face and in utter disbelief cried out within:

'Oh my God. Oh no, not here!'

I was undergoing a transfiguration and I had no power to stop it. There were only two other people in the restaurant – two women – and both were watching this metamorphosis in jaw-dropping disbelief. It must have looked like a scene from a science fiction movie as my face turned into that of a wizened old Native American Indian with long white hair, yellow teeth and thick, lined skin. A moment before they had been looking at a rotund, smooth-faced guy with short, dark hair.

Normally, a spirit or spirit guide would ask a psychic's permission to transfigure – the spirit would ask, simply, 'Can I use you?' Then, in order for the transfiguration to take place the psychic has to agree and give permission. My wise and trusted spirit guide White Cloud had seen fit, without my consent, to transfigure his appearance onto me. It was his lesson to me for drinking too much – to show that he could do what he liked because my hangover had rendered me out of control. He wanted me to be a sober psychic.

Horrified by the shock I'd given the other diners and desperate to regain control and restore my appearance I rushed from the restaurant into the foyer. I was confused and fearful and could only imagine what my fellow diners might think or say about me. As sternly as I could, I asked White Cloud to go away:

'Please go, White Cloud. Please, not here. I understand what you are saying to me.'

Thankfully, my guide did as I asked and I looked like my old self again. I knew, then, that I had to give up drinking alcohol if I wanted to continue as a medium. It was not hard to make the choice and since that day I haven't touched a drop of booze. I used to enjoy going out for a drink with the lads at my local but I no longer do that; I could find myself in a pub, half-cut, with everyone's spirit world relatives trying to come through to me when I can't control it – no laughing matter, believe me. As White Cloud demonstrated, with alcohol in me I don't have the required control over the spirits – it's much the same principle as 'don't drink and drive'. These days when I'm out socializing I drink Diet Coke – gallons of the stuff.

Returning to transfiguration, I know exactly what 'Can I use you?' means and have twice before given permission for the spirits to come through for transfiguration; I just click a switch in my mind to allow it to happen.

The last time I agreed to it was when I was giving some healing to a girl from Norfolk called Emma. Her sister had died when both siblings were in their early teens; her father, who was American and an alcoholic, had died some three or four years before I met her.

All was going well until, suddenly, Emma freaked out when her father's face was transfigured onto mine She looked at me and screamed, 'Don't do this, I don't like it.' The last thing I wanted to do was upset her, so I quickly told the spirit to leave – and it did – and I made profuse apologies to Emma.

On the second occasion, transfiguration occurred when I was with a friend who's marriage had, I knew, been an unhappy one. The face of her father, who had passed over a few years before, became superimposed on mine and I then repeated the exact words he'd spoken thirty years earlier on her wedding day, telling her it was not too late to change her mind and cancel it. She screamed in horror at me, too, and called me every name under the sun. Again, I quickly asked the spirit to leave.

On both occasions I had given the spirits permission to transfigure me, but I no longer work that way when giving readings. I know of one psychic who allows transfiguration with every reading, but I've concluded that it's too scary and upsetting for those I am reading for and I don't want to make them feel that way.

My psychic ability has also had a detrimental effect on my hearing. I had always had excellent hearing until around the time I turned professional when I noticed I was too often having to say, 'I beg your pardon?' and needing to ask people to 'speak up'. I tried out various hearing aids, but couldn't believe how noisy everything became when I was wearing them. Concerned that these overblown noises might interfere with messages from the spirit world, I soon gave up on hearing aids. These days, people assume I'm rudely ignoring them if they speak to me and I walk right past. The fact is, I simply have not heard their greeting.

Perhaps the spirits have dulled my sense of hearing because they want me to hear them more clearly than I do humans. That way, with minimal distraction, we can communicate all the better. It is said that when you lose one of your five senses then others compensate by becoming more acute. For example, a blind person's hearing may become sharper than that of a sighted person's. My deafness may be helping to sharpen my paranormal powers. It is surely more than mere coincidence that it happened when I turned professional.

Interestingly, during a hearing test I was asked who taught me to lip read.

'I don't lip read,' I replied.

'Oh, but you do,' they insisted.

This was news to me, but the medics tell me I have somehow taught myself to lip read. It is, however, something that came naturally and I wasn't even aware I could do it. Jagna or White Cloud must have helped me; they always have my wellbeing at heart.

★   ★   ★

Twelve years ago I sustained a whiplash injury in a car accident which has left me with trapped nerves in my neck and back – had I known the extent to which I'd continue to suffer I would never have accepted such a small insurance payout.

Incidentally, when I had the car accident I'm convinced the spirits (I don't know if either Jagna or White Cloud were involved but whichever spirit it was, I'm eternally grateful) had a hand in preventing an even worse injury – in fact, they saved my life. I used to drive regularly on a stretch of road between Newmarket and a quaintly named village called Six Mile Bottom and for some inexplicable reason, would see car lights in the same place every night – and then they would vanish. The funny thing was, they were just car lights, but without the car; I never saw a car.

One night, I was driving that route when I saw a car coming toward me on my side of the road – it looked as if we would crash, head-on, and I was shitting myself, but he just clipped my wing mirror. The force of the impact, however, was enough to shatter my side window. The car had hit me at the exact spot I always saw the mysterious lights and I have never seen them since. I shivered as I realized they must have been a warning from the spirit world that something was going to happen to me there.

The driver didn't stop and I was livid. I turned my car around to follow him, but he'd spun off the road and crashed into a tree. I rushed over to see if I could help, but for his female passenger it was too late. That is the only time I've ever seen a dead body and the vision will remain with me for the rest of my life. I saw the woman's spirit rise from her body and pass through to the spirit world. Rooted to the spot, I watched the tiniest pinprick of light leave her body, whoosh up into the air like a shooting star, then it was gone. I had never seen anything like it, and it unravelled the belief I'd always held that a spirit left the body in the form of its human figure – which I'd based on how I always see spirits before my eyes – fully formed, as if human.

When the police came to take a statement two days later they said they knew already that I had not been at fault. The policeman said the other driver had been overtaking at 110 mph and had I not been already driving on the grass verge at the time I wouldn't have had time to react and avoid the accident. He did, however, want to know why I had been driving on the grass verge and I told him I had no clue – I hadn't realized I was. He told me how lucky I'd been – that if the other car had hit the main body of mine I'd have been dead, 'absolutely, certainly dead' he said.

Then, when he asked my profession, so he could include it on the statement, and I told him, 'psychic medium', he said:

'Ah, now I understand why you were on the grass verge. They were certainly looking after you that night.'

And he was right. The car would have been a write off

and I'd be dead, but for my guardian angel watching over me that night.

How many psychics have had repeated death threats from an irate husband when, after a reading, his wife was able to tell him she now knew he was cheating on her? It happened to me. And 'irate' is putting it mildly because the man who hounded me was, in my opinion, furious to the extent that he was crazed. For nine months I was subjected to threatening phone calls from him; it was like being stalked.

At first, he made silent calls – phoned but didn't speak – and I really got sick of them. Later, I would pick up the phone and he'd say, 'You bastard,' no more, no less. And this would happen up to ten times a day. The calls were unpleasant and disruptive, so I reported them to the police. They told me to change my number, but when it's a business number it's just not practical.

The calls then became more sinister and threatening. I remember answering one night and listening in shock to his chilling voice saying:

'You bastard. You told my wife that she is an angel. I'm going to stab you and you won't even see it coming.'

At that stage I had no idea what he was talking about and I never had a chance to ask because he always hung up as soon as he finished speaking. The calls continued with the same threats repeated again and again. His words made me shiver and I worried whether he was a harmless nutter or a serious psychotic.

Eventually, I did manage to speak to him. He had said, in his usual menacing tone, 'I'm going to get you and you won't even see it coming. I'm going to wait until you are doing a show somewhere and I'm going to stab you in the back of the neck.' I decided to call his bluff:

'Here's my address, come and meet me right now,' I said and blurted out my address.

I'm easy enough to find, anyway. Of course, he never did come to see me but he kept on phoning. Finally, one day, I managed to say to him:

'So I told your wife you were having an affair?'

'Yes, you bastard,' he replied.

'Well you were, weren't you?'

'That's got fuck all to do with you and you've got no right to call my wife an angel.'

'Well,' I countered. 'She's more than a fucking angel for putting up with you, isn't she?'

With that, he hung up and that was the last I ever heard from him.

How would you feel if some guy you had never met before came up to you out of the blue and said, 'Excuse me love, I'm a psychic and I've got a message for you from your mum/dad, or whoever, in the spirit world'? The chances are you would tell them to get lost and I wouldn't blame you. As a rule, this is an approach that I avoid out of courtesy and because it is intrusive. The stranger may not want to speak to me and, in addition, will most likely regard me as a total nutcase. There are, however, exceptions to every rule as was the case here:

I was standing by the frozen chips in Newmarket's Netto supermarket when, loud and clear, I heard a voice in my head – not something that usually happens when I am out shopping. It was an elderly man and his tone was urgent:

'I'm Harry. I died eight days ago. That's my wife and daughter behind you. Would you please give them a message?'

I told him straight, 'No. I don't do that.'

But he was insistent that his message was important and I realized I wouldn't get any peace unless I agreed to pass it on. Harry's spirit had identified two women, one in her sixties, the other in her eighties, and explained his dilemma:

'Since I died they've been tearing their hair out trying to find the will and the insurance policy. They're upset and anxious about it. Please tell them where they are, please help them.'

When Harry told me where he had hidden the documents I had to agree that his wife and daughter had no chance of finding them, so I took a deep breath, walked up to the older of the two women and said:

'Excuse me, are you Harry's wife?'

'Yes, dear, did you know him?' she asked, smiling at me.

'No, but I have just been speaking to him.'

'That's impossible, he died eight days ago.'

'Yes, he told me that – I'm a psychic. He's telling me you can't find the will and the insurance policy.'

Harry's wife and daughter looked at each other in disbelief but, at the same time, confirmed that they had been searching the house from top to bottom, without any luck. I then passed on what Harry's spirit had told me:

'Lift up the floor boards in the airing cupboard and there you will find a tin with a Scottish piper on its lid. The documents are in the tin.'

Bemused but very excited, the women went straight home to investigate. I'd given them my number and asked them to let me know what happened. Three hours later I received a call:

'You were right. I can't believe it, I have never in my life known anything like it. The papers were just where you said, where Harry told you.'

They told everyone they knew how I'd helped them and as a result my phone was red hot for weeks: I reckon I booked in 500 readings following Harry's message.

Something similar happened when I stopped off one day at a pub in the Midlands for a bite to eat. I was sitting near a group of four people and kept hearing a man's spirit telling me he wanted me to give a message to his wife – she was one of the women in the group and he described her clearly.

I tried to ignore him but he was not going to let me be, so, reluctantly, I approached the woman and explained who I was and that her husband had a message for her. Rather than pass it on there and then, I gave her my card and left her to call if she chose. She did contact me and, though the message appeared unremarkable, it was obviously important to her husband.

Obviously, I would never charge for an unsolicited reading. Indeed, should anyone ever tell you they've a message from the spirit world and want you to pay for it, don't: it's one of the oldest scams in the book.

A word, now, about confidentiality. Many people have asked – and continue to ask – for my thoughts about what might have happened in the case of Madeleine McCann. Madeleine was about to turn four when she went missing without trace in May 2007 while on holiday with her family in Portugal. I am also asked frequently whether I have contacted her parents with regard to their daughter's disappearance. The answer is 'no' and I would not dream of doing so.

The McCanns have never asked for my advice, and if they did, whatever we might discuss would be confidential. Out of respect for the family's privacy I, therefore, refuse to publicly discuss this very sad case. The McCanns have been inundated by approaches from psychics – some will be charlatans – and I have no intention of adding to the list. I offer psychic advice only when invited to do so by whoever will be its recipient. I treat all my clients with the utmost respect and everyone I read for knows they can trust me to keep their confidence. My reputation depends on such principles.

Over the years I have read for clients rich and poor, famous and not so famous, the simply curious and those in desperate need – in short, a very mixed bag. The examples that follow illustrate the wide variety of people I encounter in the course of my work.

I was reading in Milton Keynes one night when a 28-year-old woman sat with me. Her husband had been killed in a car crash and he had no insurance. The woman, I realized, was destitute. She had three sons, all under the age of eight, she was struggling to cope with her husband's death and struggling financially.

I read for her and her husband's spirit came straight through to me. His wife was overjoyed. At the end of the reading, I touched her on the hand and said, 'That's on me,' but she was so happy with the reading that no matter how much I protested she insisted she wanted to pay.

I really did not want to take any money from her. Then, inspired, I suggested she give me ten pounds: she handed me a tenner, I handed it straight back to her and said, 'Now, will you please do me a favour and get your lovely boys some sweets with this?'

Her face lit up, and a tear trickled down her cheek as she thanked me.

Conversely, I have clients for whom money is no object. I was invited to Malaysia to read for a woman in Kuala Lumpur: she offered to pay for the flight plus £10,000 for the reading. While it was an offer that most psychics wouldn't refuse I wasn't even tempted: first, money, as I said earlier, is not the motivation for my work, and second, I was nervous about flying and had never been in an aeroplane. I told the woman that my diary was full and I, therefore, could not find time to travel.

Undaunted and determined she decided she would, in that case, come to me – and she did. One week later, at the appointed hour, she turned up on my doorstep. It's remarkable the lengths some people will go to for a reading and I couldn't help thinking what a far cry from her accustomed multimillion-pound luxury my old council house must seem.

The reading confirmed the woman's suspicion that her husband was having an affair with his secretary. She assured me that this confirmation justified her journey, that she would now divorce him and then she left – very satisfied.

While on the subject of my wealthier clients, worthy of

a mention is a group of four Russian women. They fly in twice a year from Moscow for a reading, bringing an interpreter to translate for them. This quartet of designer-clad forty-somethings are blatantly and ostentatiously rich – think diamonds as big as grapes. One of the group makes and sells jewellery and through something to do with her business had crossed swords with the Russian mafia. On the subject of poverty in Russia I was told:

'Only the poor are poor, we are the richest people in the world.'

Wealthy as they are, they ask the same questions as many other women do about life and love. And they pay the same amount everyone else does for their readings with me. Prince or pauper, my rates are set and I aim to be affordable to everyone.

My reputation extends far beyond these shores with clients from places including the Channel Islands, mainland Europe and even Australia. Recently I had an e-mail from someone in Australia who is coming to England over Christmas and wants to book a reading while he is here. How they all track me down I'm never quite sure.

I read for a number of celebrities, too, from the pop world, film and TV. But I cannot emphasize too strongly that, for me, a client is a client is a client – all are equal in my eyes and they can all rely on me to be straight with them in every aspect of my work.

The truth is key. Sadly, not all psychics are honest and some – usually in an attempt to attract clients – either imply or even make false claims that they have read for this or that celebrity. Consider, for example, the number of psychics who claim to have read for Princess Diana. We knew that the late princess had consulted psychics but if she'd gone to the number that claim to have read for her she would have been seeing a psychic every day of her life.

Everyone has secrets and for that reason I insist only one person sits with me for a reading. People may want a friend or relative to sit in with them but, as a general rule, I don't allow it. When reading for two or more people at the same time there's a risk that the clients' energies will converge and spirits may then get them mixed up. As I said, we all have secrets and secrets have a habit of coming out during a reading.

I had been booked to read for two women at a house in Cambridgeshire. Both women were in their early thirties, they insisted they were best friends and wanted me to read them together. I wasn't keen, and explained the reasons why.

Both women were adamant they had no secrets, 'We know everything there is to know about each other,' and pleaded with me to read them together. So, much against my better judgement, I agreed to do as they asked. It was all fairly run-of-the-mill stuff – at least what I told them was pretty mundane and they both seemed happy enough with that.

At the end of the evening the woman whose house it was took me to the door and said:

'Thanks, Dennis, that was brilliant. I told you we knew everything about each other.'

And I looked her straight in the face and said:

'Yes, you do, don't you? But she doesn't know you're shagging her husband, does she?'

My host nearly died with shock:

'How do you know that?'

'It's my job to know,' I said.

Obviously I couldn't say anything about this during my reading and I made sure I told her well out of her so-called best friend's earshot. I'm blunt and honest but, on occasions such as this one, also compassionate and tactful.

As soon as I started my reading Jagna told me about the affair – she doesn't keep people's secrets from me – so, I then had to filter all the incoming information from the spirits. I didn't dare open my mouth in sync with spirits as I normally do for fear of letting the cat out of the bag. It is not a good way to work at all: it gives my own mind too much time to think and this makes the reading more haphazard.

A son's secret reached his mother's ears during a reading

at a psychic fair in Kent. The mother, alone, was sitting with me. Her husband came straight through and after telling me he'd been a builder and died when he fell through a roof, he started talking about his fourteen year-old son.

'He wants to talk to his son,' I said. 'He is telling me he's here.'

'Yes, he is, he is sitting out in the car. He doesn't want to come in,' she replied.

She did, however, go and fetch her son and they sat together with me. Normally I would never do a straight face to face reading for someone under sixteen, but when it's a question of a spirit specifically trying to contact them, rather than the child wanting to initiate a search into the unknown themselves, then as long as they're happy and I personally feel comfortable with the situation, I'm willing to make exceptions. His father's spirit started talking about football and how proud he was of his son who had just been signed up by a top football club. Mother and son were ecstatic that the boy's father knew about this.

But next, the father wanted me to pass a clear message to his wayward son:

'And you can stop smoking the puff.'

The mother was furious. She clipped her son around the ear and he nearly fell off the chair. I was aghast. She looked at me and said:

'You have been so right on everything else. If my husband

has told you that boy is smoking cannabis, then he is, and I am not putting up with that.'

The boy sat there, nonplussed. He didn't deny it. In hindsight, I should have read with the boy alone.

No one can pull the wool over the eyes of my spirit guides. A strikingly beautiful young woman came to me for a reading. There was nothing untoward in the reading but Jagna had told me she was a porn star. We'd got along well, so I decided to tell her that I knew what she did for a living. She just looked at me and smiled:

'I see I can't keep any secrets from you, Dennis, can I?'

'No, my love,' I told her. 'No one can.'

Then there was the very well-to-do looking girl who came to sit with me wearing a Burberry coat and clutching a matching bag. 'She's a hooker,' said Jagna. I laughed to myself because never in a million years would I have thought it of this very posh looking woman. I wasn't quite sure how to put this to the client. So I tested the water and asked:

'You work in a very old profession, don't you?'

She looked up in total surprise without replying.

'Is there much trade for you around here then?' I continued.

'You know, don't you?' she said.

She was, it transpired, a call girl working the very top end of the market.

So, no such thing as a secret in the spirit world.

★ ★ ★

People often ask if I see when someone is going to die. The short answer, here, is that it isn't easy, but neither is it impossible. My spirit guides are very careful about the information I have in this circumstance, as the following two cases will demonstrate.

I went to do some readings a few months ago in Surrey. This came about after I had been reading at a psychic fair where I heard about a woman, Sue, who'd had a really bad reading from another psychic. Sue's nose was in bandages following major plastic surgery to treat a genetic disorder but the reader, guessing incorrectly, assumed she'd been in a car accident and said so.

As I left the show I spotted Sue and, sorry that she'd been let down by the poor reading, gave her my card and said, 'If you want a reading, call me. It's on me, there's no charge.' As always, if I offer a reading I don't charge. Sue thanked me and, later, called to take up my offer.

In order to make it worth my while, she'd offered to get together a few people for readings at her home in Surrey, and when I turned up one of Sue's guests was already there, waiting for her reading. My instinct told me that I should not read for this person.

I gave Sue the reading I'd promised her and, by then, four more people had turned up. I looked, again, at the woman who had arrived first and knew I couldn't read for her, though I didn't know why. I could sense from her energies that there was something really heavy and bad around her. It was a very strong feeling which I could not ignore and I decided I didn't want to be the bearer of any bad news.

But if I read for Sue's other guests, how could I avoid reading for this particular woman? I could think of only one way out and feigned illness. I said I'd been feeling rough all day and I'd have to go home.

Two weeks later I learned that the woman had died: she was only in her late forties but had suffered a massive heart attack. So, that was the reason I hadn't wanted to read for her: there was no way I could break that news. I'm glad I didn't know. It was, also, the spirits' way of protecting her.

Another interesting example of how I do not see impending death as clearly as I can other events took place a few years ago. I was just outside London, reading for a group of young women. The last reading of the evening was for a 34-year-old woman called Liz and I told her how I couldn't see any change in her life:

'Liz, this is really boring, but you've got everything. You've got a lovely lifestyle, a husband with his own car dealership and two lovely children. Obviously life is going to be the same for you because I'm seeing nothing here.'

Two weeks later Liz phoned and asked if I would read for her husband, David. I agreed and arranged to read for him:

'I can see you on a beach next year and you really are deliriously happy,' I told David. 'It's Barbados, or somewhere like that – somewhere like the Caribbean. I can see you on the beach with this lady, walking hand in hand, so it looks like you and Liz are going to be very happy.'

Three weeks after I read for David, Liz got up off the sofa and had a brain haemorrhage and died. That explained why I hadn't seen any change in her life – but I had not been shown her death. Once again, the spirits protected both parties from the knowledge of imminent death. I still get the shivers when I remember these two cases.

David, incidentally, did walk on a beach in an exotic location. Months after Liz died, he fell in love with someone and one year later they married – on a tropical beach.

While I have never had advance knowledge of anyone's imminent death that's not to say that I can't warn someone to change something in their life in order to benefit their health. For example, during one woman's reading my clairsentience and Jagna were telling me that she needed urgent medical attention:

'You've got a stomach problem, haven't you?' I suggested.

'Yes, I have, a little bit,' said the woman and she added that she wasn't too bothered about it.

Knowing it was, in fact, serious, I made clear my concern and asked her to promise to see a doctor a soon as possible. She continued to try and brush me off while I continued to try and convince her that it was imperative she see a doctor. Finally, she agreed:

'Okay, I'll go and see my doctor, I make you that promise.'

Six months later she phoned to thank me. She had been diagnosed with cancer but the early diagnosis had, the doctor told her, saved her life.

I regard my ability to see, hear and feel spirit as a very special and valuable gift. It mirrors in me not only the emotions but also any physical pain suffered by another. Reading for a lady, once, I experienced such terrible chest pain I fell to the floor in agony, but the pain passed in an instant, I picked myself up and felt fine again.

'Did your husband have a heart attack?' I asked.

He did, indeed, I was told.

'I thought so!'

Sometimes, the spirits come on a little too strong.

I don't see just doom and gloom, there is happiness – and love – in store for many of the people I read for and it always gives me great joy to pass on good news. Here is how I know that the spirit world can play Cupid:

I was reading for a woman in her fifties when the spirit of a boy came through. I could see that he was aged around twenty and that he was very high spirited. He opened with:

'I'm Marc, spelled with a curly 'C', not a kicking 'K'.'

Then Marc's spirit said, 'She's going out with my mate.'

I wondered what was going on. Did she, perhaps, have a toy boy? I passed on what his spirit had told me and asked if I'd understood correctly. She explained that yes, she was going out with Marc's mate – his mate at work, who was the same age as my client. That cleared up any confusion on my part.

Then, Marc had another message for her:

'He says it's about time you said "yes".'

'Ask him "yes" to what?'

Quick as a flash, Marc's spirit said:

'He's asked her to marry him so many times and each time she says no. Tell her I want her to say "yes". Tell her I want her to go home tonight and say "yes".'

Six months later I received an invitation to the wedding.

When I tell a woman she's going to meet a tall, dark, handsome man and get married, I mean it. There are times, of course, when the man in question might be short, bald and not so handsome, but who cares as long as true love is found. Some women worry that they will never meet their Mr Right and that romance and marriage will never happen for them – but the happy outcomes I've predicted have come good.

I read for a middle aged woman who had had huge troubles in her relationships with men. She was single and desperate to find love. I told her it would happen one day, and who her ideal partner would be. Two years later she phoned me, out of the blue – I couldn't even remember reading for her; it's impossible to remember every person I have seen and what I have told them. Why was she ringing me? She sounded almost hostile when she spoke:

'You read for me two years ago. You told me that I was going to meet a South African with a German accent, and that I would marry him in South Africa and we would be happy ever after.'

I held the phone thinking, 'Oh shit, I've got this one wrong, and I've got a bollocking coming.' But then she said:

'I'm actually at the airport at the moment. I did meet this South African and he'd lived in Germany for a while. We're on our way to South Africa to get married.'

I felt a huge surge of relief as I heard her laughing – she knew she'd had me worried – then she told me how impressed she was with how things had worked out just as I'd predicted.

It is always fantastic, and very reassuring, to get feedback such as this, especially on something so specific. For example, I'd done a reading for a woman in which I'd told her who her Mr Right was going to be. Five years later she was back, sitting in front of me with a huge grin on her face:

'Dennis, I had to let you know that everything you told me five years ago turned out to be true. I am just amazed by it.

'I told you I was going to live in Barbados, but you said,

"No, it's Grenada, you will get a house in Grenada." I remember arguing with you about this until I was blue in the face. You told me I would meet a Grenadian guy that you'd expect would be black, but he wouldn't be black. And you told me he'd have stunning eyes.'

I was listening keenly to every word she spoke. She continued:

'Well, I have met him, he is a white Grenadian and he does have the most stunningly beautiful eyes.'

Of course, I was thrilled with her news.

I read for a woman in Aberdeen: she was a hard woman, and I mean hard. When she sat with me I looked into her stony face and said:

'Don't worry my love, there's a man coming into your life.'

'There's no fucking man coming in my life. I don't want any fucking man in my life,' she said.

I was positive a man would be coming into her life, I even gave her the date on which he would phone her and was able to add:

'You already have a connection with this man. He's not a stranger, but someone you've known in the past.'

She would have none of it.

A year later, I returned to Aberdeen and, again, she sat with me. I didn't recognize her until she reminded me about her earlier reading – this time she was smiling and her expression had softened. At half past eleven at night on the date I had given her a boy she had known when she was sixteen phoned her and the two of them were now living together. I gave her a big hug.

I love giving people good news, but the day I make something up just so a punter can go home feeling better about themselves is the day I retire as a professional psychic. I don't bullshit. I say it as I see it, the good and the bad.

It's every dad's dream to give his daughter away on her wedding day and, even though John was in the spirit world, he wanted to be there for his beloved daughter Mary when she tied the knot with James. James and Mary, you will remember, live in Nottinghamshire and now run a business together. I first came across Mary at a psychic fair. I was among a group of psychics, laying out our Tarot cards, waiting for visitors to decide which of us they wanted to sit with. Mary looked toward me yet she appeared apprehensive. She wandered off, then returned. I could see she was still dithering but felt she would sit with me – sooner or later. I often see that happening with clients, especially those who have something playing on their mind. Eventually she took the plunge:

'Okay, what kept you so long?' I asked.

'This is the first time I have ever done anything like this,' she said. 'I've come along with a friend and I'm not sure what this is all about and whether I even believe in it. I'd like to have a chat.'

I asked if there was anything specific she would like to talk about and she said, 'Yes, a family member who has died.' Then I asked if she had brought anything that had belonged to that person – this helps to make a much stronger connection with the person's spirit. 'Not exactly,' said Mary. 'But I do have a photo of my mother and father on their wedding day.'

'Please don't show it to me, turn it upside down on the table and let me 'hover' over it and have a bit of a feel – see what I can pick up.'

As I held my hands over the photo I sensed immediately that her mother was still alive but that her father had passed over; I picked up his voice in spirit:

'It was sudden, wasn't it?' I asked. Then, suddenly, I gripped my arms across my chest and slumped across the table:

'Oh my God, I can hardly breathe. My chest is really tight.'

Poor Mary, apprehensive to start with, looked on in horror. The pain stopped and I said:

'It was his heart wasn't it? That's the pain I was feeling just then. I can see he'd been suffering for the last few years of his life. I can tell you now, my love, that he is free from pain.'

Mary confirmed that six months earlier, at the age of sixty-four, her father had died suddenly after a severe heart attack. John had not been in good health but his family had expected him to live for another three or four years, at least.

'He wants me to say thank you from him for the six roses at his funeral, he says that was very sweet.'

Mary gasped at this revelation:

'When we went to the funeral, I took six yellow roses with me and gave one to each member of the family. I'm so glad he liked them.'

'Darling, he loved those roses. And he also wants you to know he has joined his brother Richard and sister Anne who passed over several years before.'

The reading gave Mary not only comfort but also a degree of closure on her father's death – she felt a weight had been lifted from her:

'My dad died so suddenly that it really shocked me. I have been so sad about not saying goodbye to him. It has been so wonderful to speak to him through you. I really feel my dad is in a good place and that he is okay.' I did not see Mary for a few years until she came for a reading three months before she was due to marry James in October 2002. She had made all her preparations but there was one very important plan I felt she had to change:

'Your dad is saying very firmly that only he is going to give you away, he doesn't want anyone to do it – he is going to be there with you. He keeps repeating it,' I told her.

'What! I've already asked my boss to give me away. He's

a father figure to me and he's helped me through so much since dad passed over. How am I going to tell him he doesn't need to because a psychic has told me that my dead father is going to do the job instead?'

'I don't know, love,' I said. 'But it will all be fine on the day, I know it.'

Because her dad's spirit had been so emphatic, Mary decided to respect his wishes. She explained to her boss that as it was impossible for her father to give her away, she would prefer that no one did.

The big day came and when Mary married James at one of Nottinghamshire's beautiful stately homes, she could feel her father's presence by her side. John kept his promise and was with her as she walked past the rows of guests to stand with James before the registrar. She felt her father give her away.

'He was by my side the whole time,' Mary told me. 'I felt his presence close to me as I walked across that room, I really didn't feel I was on my own.'

For the bride, John's spiritual presence had made a wonderful day even better. He had known James and thought him the perfect match for his daughter – he also used to say that he'd be proud to have him as a son.

As I'd predicted, the wedding went without a hitch. And there was a wonderful surprise for the happy couple within their wedding photos: they hadn't noticed a silhouette in the background. But I did. We looked closely and picked out, behind the registrar, the silhouette of a man wearing a flat cap. Mary instantly recognized the shape of the cap: 'That's just what my dad used to wear.'

Living with my psychic ability clearly impacts on my life. However, my *work* as a professional psychic involves no more or less than many other people's jobs do. I try to do my job well, I am paid for my work, and I deal with whatever each day brings.

My work demands that I empathize with the people I read for but once a reading is over I revert to being myself – the same principle applies to professionals such as doctors, nurses, social workers, teachers and so on. There are days when one reading might be for someone who has experienced an obviously serious trauma, while the next is for something that appears trivial. But I never judge anyone – one person's mole hill is another's mountain.

When I'm reading for someone and sharing their deepest and most private thoughts, making their spine tingle as I reveal information about their life which no other living soul is aware of, it might seem to them that I know everything about them. But no one on this earth can ever know that much and the spirits don't know it all, either.

Wichita: in the Wake of a Killer

It was a glorious hot day in Wichita, Kansas – not a cloud in the sky. I stepped inside the shabby, timber-framed bungalow and quickly scanned the room. I was overwhelmed by a sense of brooding darkness, my skin turned cold and I knew this was a house of evil where acts of terrible depravity had taken place.

I winced at the distinctive, sickly smell of cat shit. The room was filthy and littered with empty Coke cans. Clothes lay piled up in corners where they'd been dumped. Whoever normally occupied this house was living in squalor.

My visit here in September 2004 was the subject of a documentary and the cameraman and his soundman were following my every move. My psychic powers enabled me to see what they could not – the sickening murders which happened in this place thirty years ago.

Pictures flashed in my mind's eye showing the corpses of a man and a woman. They were the most horrible images but I came straight out with it and told the crew:

'I can see two dead people on a bed, one with their tongue hanging out.'

The afternoon sun burst through the front windows and guided me toward the next room. Here was another horrific scene, one which will live with me for the rest of my life. The camera zoomed in on me and the crew held their breath waiting for me to speak:

'I feel this was where a little boy has died; with a hood on his head.'

As I said the words, my hands grew ice-cold. Then the room turned cold, spine-chillingly cold. The images which flashed in my mind's eye were so vivid, as if the killings had taken place only moments before.

Retired police detective Bernie Drowatzky was going from room to room with us. He had worked on the infamous case we were revisiting and had therefore been to this house many times. He'd seen those bodies a matter of hours after their death and this visit was bringing back grim memories of the string of perversely brutal murders that shocked everyone who heard of them.

I described where I saw each body and Bernie nodded silent confirmation. I followed him down some steps into the cellar, ducked and looked to the right. In an instant I knew this was where the worst evil had taken place. Cold seeped into my bones and I shivered, then I shivered again and went into a deep, spiritual trance. Bernie was saying something but his words weren't reaching me. When I'm in contact with the spirit world I can listen only to the spirits speaking in my head or focus on the messages I hear, feel and see with my psychic powers:

'I can see a little girl hanging from a sewer pipe. I can see her knickers around her ankles and there is semen on her body.'

The camera held me in close-up, the mic set to pick up every word:

'I feel she had been taped to a chair and forced to watch the rest of her family being murdered.'

And I could feel her wanting to die as she hung from the pipe, hands bound behind her back and her feet just a few inches from the ground. I described the girl's sheer terror and helplessness while she hung there, not knowing what her fate might be. Through clairsentience I could feel what she had felt and through clairvoyance see the torture she had suffered. This little girl, Josephine Otero, was eleven years old. The four members of the Otero family were the killer's first victims.

Tears poured down my face, I couldn't stop them and neither did I want to. I sobbed and sobbed while these four cruel deaths replayed in my mind and asked myself what kind of bastard could kill two innocent kids and their parents so brutally? And why?

Then the most extraordinary thing happened; something I have never experienced before or since. One moment I was feeling Josephine Otero's suffering, the next the killer's depravity: his lust, his arousal, his despicable perversion. I entered the soul of the killer. This metamorphosis plunged me into deep darkness where only wickedness and brutality exist. I had entered a hell created specifically for monsters such as this. I felt what he felt when he tortured and killed Josephine. He was lingering on within me.

I can never forget that experience, what was imposed on me was horrific and for almost six months I remained subject to flashbacks – consumed by the same feelings whenever I thought about what I'd seen in that cellar. I have no clue what caused it to happen, trapped energy, perhaps, but I do not know: I wondered if he was gloating, then in my kinder moments I wondered if he wanted forgiveness – all I am sure of is that it was the worst spiritual experience I have ever had and it took me a long time to recover.

The flashbacks stopped and my nightmare came to an end when the killer was finally arrested after a protracted thirty-one-year murder investigation. I can't tell how happy I was when Dennis Rader was arrested on 25 February 2005. The killer's true identity had remained elusive throughout the entire investigation – he had been known to police and public as the BTK Strangler or BTK, an acronym he gave himself based on the method by which he murdered his victims: bind, torture, kill. Rader pleaded guilty and was convicted of ten murders committed between 1974 and 1991. I, however, believe he may have killed at least sixteen times, but that he's only admitted to ten murders to take advantage of a loophole in US law. Between 1974 and 1991, the State of Kansas had abolished the death penalty. In the US you can only ever receive the maximum punishment that was in place at the time of the crime you committed, so even though the death penalty has since been reinstated, it can't be applied retroactively unless he confesses to a murder that took place when it *was* on the statute books. As I was to find out, he is a very cunning man, though that didn't stop him being caught eventually. On 18 August 2005, he was sentenced to ten terms of life imprisonment – 175 years behind bars with no possibility of parole.

Prior to my visit there in Autumn 2004 I had never heard of Wichita, let alone known where it was. The story of why I went there began earlier that year at a psychic reading party hosted by a young woman named Julie at her home in London.

The reading I gave my host revealed some sad and unexpected news. Jagna told me that Julie's grandmother was very ill to the extent that during the previous night she had required emergency resuscitation. Julie was incredulous, certain that her mother would have told her such news:

'I'm telling you love, your grandmother will be dead by Friday. She died last night, but was resuscitated.'

Julie remained unconvinced but, an hour later, was telling me:

'I've spoken to my mother on the phone. You were right, Dennis, you were spot on. My grandmother died twice last night and was resuscitated both times.'

Julie's grandmother died that week, on Wednesday night.

When Julie booked me for her psychic reading party she was fully aware of my connection with the Wells family – by then my reputation as the 'Soham psychic' was well established. Following the reading I had given her, Julie had been so impressed by my skill as a psychic that she offered to represent me:

'Dennis, I would like to be your agent. I know you have great talent and I'm sure it won't be long before the work is pouring in.'

I didn't need much arm twisting and joined her agency, JEM Sports & Media Management, based at the Elstree film studios in Hertfordshire. It was as simple as that. JEM boasted an impressive client list – including actor and entertainer Shane Ritchie who I'm a big fan of – so, I was in good hands.

Julie – Jules, as I like to call her – put me in touch with

a TV company planning a documentary to be made in the US. I was – intentionally – to be kept in the dark: I was told that the producer, Mark, wanted to test out my psychic ability on a mystery project and that I would be going to America for two weeks – though I didn't know where in America. When I'm doing something like this I actually prefer to be kept 'bubble-wrapped'. On one level, it presents more of a challenge, but more than that it means I can apply my psychic ability free of any outside influences. Prior exposure to a case can throw up all kinds of misleading clues and blind alleys which stop me operating to my full capacity and prejudice my conclusions. Confident in my powers and knowing I can always rely on Jagna, I agreed to give it my best shot and that was how, at the ripe old age of fifty, I went on my first trip abroad.

A novice traveller, rarely slipping over the Cambridgeshire border, here I was, bound for the US to work with a bunch of people I didn't know from Adam. 'I must be stark, staring mad,' I thought. Mark was already Stateside and John, the soundman, and I were to fly out together to join him. John and I met for the first time at Heathrow airport:

'Hey, Dennis, we're off to Chicago,' he said.

Chicago, to me, meant gangsters, that was all I knew about the place. I wondered if this mystery documentary might be something about the Mob – that would certainly be different from what I normally came across in Cambridgeshire. I was intrigued.

I had been very nervous about flying but was relieved to discover that, apart from feeling pretty squeezed into my seat, it didn't really bother me.

As soon as we landed in Chicago, John announced we were now flying on to Wichita. 'Bloody hell,' I thought. We'd been on the go all day and I couldn't believe there was farther still to go. I was pissed off, too, because my nebulizer had just been nicked. I left my case for five minutes and some lowlife stole it off the top of my bag. I have asthma so it's my lifeline because it helps me breathe.

I don't even know if those thieving buggers knew what they had pinched. They probably looked at it, thought it was a load of rubbish and just chucked it away, but I can't manage without it. Luckily, I managed to buy another one, otherwise, I'm telling you, I'd have been on the return flight.

Going through immigration I became a bit uneasy when the officer looked me straight in the eye and said:

'Are you really going to Wichita, Kansas? Are you going on vacation there?'

'No,' I replied. 'I'm not going there on holiday. I'm going there to make a documentary.'

'Ah, I knew it. No one goes to Wichita on vacation.' And she gave me a look as if to say, 'You poor old thing. Rather you than me.'

I wondered what on earth I had let myself in for but had no choice but to follow John through to internal transfers for our next departure. Chicago O'Hare airport is massive and we walked for what seemed like miles. It would be a two-hour flight to Wichita which, I had learned by then, is in America's Midwest. As for what was expected of me at our destination, John was giving away nothing:

'All will be revealed in good time,' was all he would say.

We walked onto the tarmac and I stopped dead. I pointed to the tiny plane scheduled to fly to Wichita, hoping it was a mistake or a bad dream. It was the smallest plane I had ever seen in my life:

'Bloody hell. I can't believe we're going on THAT thing.'

'I'm afraid so, Dennis. After you,' said John, pointing the way forward.

'Bugger it, no way, I can't believe I'm really going on that thing.'

John led the way, smiling. I stepped nervously into the cabin and did a quick seat-count:

'Wait 'til I tell everyone back home, they won't believe it. This plane has only got twenty seats.'

John tried to put me at ease and I soon, anyway, realized I had nothing to worry about:

'I don't like this plane,' I said. 'But if there was going to be a problem on the flight I would be the first to know and I certainly wouldn't be sitting here now.'

That made him smile and it made me feel a bit better, too, though I remained nervous as the plane took off then bobbed about in the sky. Still, I couldn't help looking to see the lie of the land below – and there were moments when it felt quite wonderful to be even closer to the spirit world.

We touched down at Wichita in the early hours. It was dark and the warm air took me by surprise as I stepped off the plane. It was September and I'd left the UK in the beginnings of typically damp autumnal weather, never thinking I'd need to pack light clothing. When Mark met us at the airport he asked if we'd had a good flight and John winked as I tried to make out it was okay. After all, it had been okay, we had reached Wichita in one piece.

With 360,000 residents Wichita is the largest city in Kansas – vast compared to my home village in Cambridgeshire, population 7,000 and that's big enough for a country-loving man like me. I like a good time, don't get me wrong, but I can have that down the pub with my mates.

The city was named after the Wichita Indians who made the area their home. With its reputation for aircraft production established since the 1920s, Wichita became an important aeroplane manufacturing centre during World War II and remains a major player in the aircraft industry today, hence its nickname, the Air Capital of America. Ironic, then, that I who had never been in a plane before and with no love for flying should end up here.

I was exhausted and couldn't stop yawning – and so relieved to have the journey behind me – that when we reached the hotel I went out like a light as soon as my head hit the pillow. Oblivious of what lay in store for me, I slept like a baby.

The next morning I awoke and was pleased to find my hotel room overlooked a park; some green relief amid the sprawling metropolis. There was a knock on my door:

'Hey, you up and ready to go? Let's get some breakfast then I need to buy some film.'

Mark was keen to make a start. My body clock hadn't begun to adjust to the time difference but I didn't mind, I was keen to find out at last what I was here for. The American breakfast lived up to its reputation as the biggest and best but there was barely time to digest it before Mark whisked John and me off in the hire car.

I looked about me as we drove. It was blisteringly hot – more than 100°F – and I wished I had brought some summer clothes with me. We were driving along the highway when Jagna's clipped voice burst into my head. She spoke fast and her tone was urgent, 'Turn right here, Dennis, turn right now,' she kept repeating. I yelled:

'Stop! Stop the car now. We've got to turn right.'

Mark slammed on the brakes and, no questions asked,

took note of the road I pointed out. He had to drive on then loop around to take the turning. My heart was racing and a familiar warm glow spread through and around my entire body: I feel this sometimes when I'm making a connection with the spirit world and it emphasizes that something very significant is about to happen. Mark, John and I were blown away; I hadn't expected my psychic abilities to begin working within minutes of leaving the hotel on day one.

I was itching to get behind the wheel and drive; I couldn't wait to find out what Jagna wanted me to see down that road, 'Come on, hurry up,' I kept telling Mark. I couldn't get there quick enough.

The road was called South Hydraulic Street – a strange name, I thought. It looked normal enough – a suburban neighbourhood with houses set back from the road – but Jagna had been so insistent that I knew there must be something very important here. Sure enough, we hadn't driven far when I began to choke: I was finding it hard to breathe as icy hands seemed to close tighter and tighter around my throat. I was burning up now and fighting for breath. I was terrified:

'Stop! Stop the car now!' I gasped.

Then I told Mark and John that I knew someone had been murdered within fifty yards of where we were at that precise moment:

'They were choked to death and I feel this has something to do with why you wanted to bring me here.'

Mark and John were speechless. Mark pulled up on the roadside; bizarrely, a hearse was parked close by. Across the road to the right, close to where I had felt myself choking, I saw a scarecrow perched on the porch of one of the houses. I stared at it and was still staring at it when we all got out of the car and Mark and John looked toward the house and Mark said:

'This is why you're here, Dennis. A woman called Shirley Vian was murdered in that house.'

Shirley Vian, a 26-year-old mother of three, was strangled by BTK at her home, 1311 South Hydraulic, on 17 March 1977: she was his sixth victim.

Mark and his crew were going to film a documentary telling the BTK story but which they also intended would 'offer police new insight into the case'. The 'new insight' it was hoped would come from me. At last, I knew what Mark expected of me and I was pleased to have been able to establish my psychic credentials at such an early stage.

The following day we made the three-hour drive out to Newkirk in Oklahoma to meet Bernie Drowatzky. Incidentally, on our way there, a lack of local knowledge cost us an instant fine when we were pulled over by the police for speeding. We were, apparently, the second lot of 'Brits' to succumb that day.

Finally, we arrived at Bernie's house. He offered a firm

handshake and a warm welcome to his home. Although in his seventies, he had kept his handsome demeanour and had an air of natural authority. His hair was thin on top and he wasn't tall, but he had big, broad shoulders and piercing eyes.

There was a framed certificate hanging on the wall and I asked him to tell the story behind it: he had negotiated the release of some hostages by offering himself in their place and had then overpowered the gunman. Bernie was not a cop you could mess around with. How many guys are brave enough to do that? That's typical Bernie. I was in awe of him when we first met and I came to respect him more and more as I got to know him. Good and kind and with a strong sense of fair play, he is one of the most remarkable men I have ever known.

He loves family life and is very happy in his retirement, though his wife was ill when we met and has since passed away, which for Bernie has been like losing his right arm. He spends a lot of time doing wood carvings. In fact, he gave me a wall plaque carved in the shape of an Indian chief with two wolves sitting beside him. It is a gift I treasure very much.

'Take it, Dennis,' Bernie insisted. 'I want you to take this back home with you to remember your time in Wichita.'

We drove to a red-neck diner called the Old Town Café, in Kaw City. I had deep reservations as we stepped inside. Run-down and ramshackle, it was a dirty old place and I couldn't work out why Bernie would take us to such a dive. I gave him the benefit of the doubt:

'The food here is the best you'll get anywhere in America,' he told us. 'This diner is so hot that people will think nothing of driving a hundred miles for one of their steaks. You should count yourself lucky we got a table.'

Bernie knew the menu off by heart and had already guessed my favourite:

'Do you like a big steak, Dennis?'

Boy, do I like a big steak? I love my food and I am particularly partial to a big, juicy steak. I could already smell meat being chargrilled and it smelled terrific. I was positively drooling. My eyes almost popped out when a thirty-six-ounce steak spilling over the edges of the plate was plonked down in front of me. I never imagined I would be able to finish it, but I did. It was the biggest steak I have ever seen and the best I've ever eaten. They say everything is bigger and better in America – well, that's certainly true of their steaks.

While we all tucked in, Bernie gave me a rundown of what he knew about BTK and explained that I would be taken to the houses where his victims had been murdered. Throughout the thirty-year investigation the police had had very little to go on. No one had a clue who BTK might be. He struck first in 1974 claiming five victims that year, then four more by 1986, and the final one in 1991. Throughout that period he would send letters, pictures and items relating to his crimes to media reporters, intended to taunt the police. The letters stopped in 1991 and nothing was heard about or from BTK until March 2004 when he resurfaced to indulge again in his one-way correspondence with the news media. The eleven letters he sent led to his arrest. BTK's renewed contact with the media and police had rekindled heightened fear among the people of Wichita. I knew I was facing a big challenge, the biggest ever by the sound of it.

As Bernie told me what was known about BTK my paranormal powers were guiding me and clairsentience enabled me to picture, instantly, what kind of man he was. I told Bernie:

'I feel this man is an ordinary guy who has a wife and family. You wouldn't notice anything strange about him if you bumped into him in the street. In fact, he is even Mr Nice Guy – ninety-five per cent of the time.'

Though the police had considered the possibility that BTK was just a normal member of the community, they were more inclined to focus their investigations on what their psychological profilers had suggested – that he was a convicted criminal. Spells in prison would explain the long gaps in time between murders. My feelings told me otherwise. This guy was not like that.

Bernie didn't dismiss anything I said; I loved the way he opened up to me about the case and trusted me as a psychic.

It was important to have that mutual respect as we were to work together closely. In fact, he told me he'd solved a missing person case with the help of a female psychic.

Bernie told me how much the Otero family's deaths sickened him:

'I couldn't believe the viciousness of them.'

He said he'd been hoping that the case would be solved before he retired, but BTK was smart. 'No matter what we've tried, or who's helped us, as far as I can see we don't seem to be any closer to tracking down this killer,' said Bernie. He said the people of Wichita wouldn't sleep soundly at night 'until that evil monster is caught' and that anything I could find out would be a great help. I promised I'd do my best.

People were, indeed, terrified the killer would strike again. They'd installed the latest security alarms in their homes and some had even bought guns. There was panic in the air and almost every man in town was regarded as a suspect.

Jagna, however, was telling me, 'He will never kill again.'

I'd been in Wichita for over a week when we visited the house where the Otero family had lived. I had never before been anywhere where so many people had been killed and was full of trepidation when we walked through the door. I could see that the guys making the documentary seemed spooked too. Looking around I could tell – it wasn't Jagna telling me, I just knew it – that various things had changed over the years. The living room had been the boy's bedroom, for example.

I'd been pleased that my clairsentience was strong. I saw the bodies as if looking at film stills, frame by frame. I'd felt hot because BTK turned up the heating when he killed. And I'd felt cold because, as I suggested to Bernie, he cooled his hands with ice so that he could enjoy the sharp contrast of his cold hands on his victim's warm throat. Bernie confirmed that police found an ice tray left out of the fridge in the kitchen.

As we moved through each room in the house Bernie confirmed the details I was picking up:

'I can see Mr Otero's shoes under the table and I feel that his wife had got out into their yard somehow, and that her nails and her fingertips were a bit ragged and worn from being dragged across the concrete – she was trying to find a hold, find something to grip on to.'

The experience was harrowing. These deaths were unspeakably cruel. Joseph junior and his parents had been strangled and bound with the cord taken from a Venetian blind. The 'hood' I'd seen over the boy's head had been, Bernie told me, a pillowcase and two plastic bags.

The evil I was conscious of when I went down into the cellar reminded me of the terror I'd known when, as a child, I'd gone to fetch drinks from the cellar of my father's pub. It was striking that even the shape of the Otero cellar was similar – down the steps then a kick to the right and the evil presence sensed toward the end; where I saw the girl, Josephine, hanging.

I could see and feel her fear and it was so horrible, so very horrible. That bastard saw it and loved it. He savoured every moment of her suffering. And he masturbated. Poor girl. She couldn't understand anything about what was going on. She didn't know who the killer was or why any of this was happening to her, or her mum and dad, or her little brother. I had felt the victims' fear and I had known BTK's sick lust. I'd hated it. I hated feeling the evil in his soul.

How can I live with such feelings? The answer is I don't – I let them go. If I stored up all that I experience I'd be totally overwhelmed and, most likely, insane. It is, in any case, impossible to remember in detail every reading and sensation. I'm doing more than a hundred readings every week; and with the best will in the world I can't even remember who I read yesterday.

What I went through in the Otero household, however, did remain in my memory and it was difficult to recover from. Bernie put his arm around my shoulder. It had stirred up ugly memories for him, too, and he had a pretty good idea how bad I was feeling. He knows he can never, ever forget this case. He described himself as a 'hardened cop' but he remains as shocked by BTK's crimes as he was when he saw the four dead bodies in 1974. The knowledge that the killer still had his freedom was almost unbearable. I wanted to help bring him to justice if I could.

I'd been thinking about the fact that BTK had managed to get into a house where there were four people and succeed in killing all of them, and my feelings, also, were telling me he had killed before. I told Bernie what was going through my mind:

'From what I've now read about him, I know BTK says that the Oteros were his first victims but I don't believe a word of it. My feelings tell me that BTK killed twice before the Oteros, and that they were single people. I think he killed sixteen times in all with the other four murders actually coming after 1991.'

On the fourth day I had returned with Bernie and the film crew to South Hydraulic. As we entered the house where Shirley Vian had died I sensed a dog barking; I also sensed that when BTK got in, the dog got out.

'This house isn't right. Something is very different,' I said.

Bernie explained that a fire had gutted the original house but that this one had been built in its place and with a similar layout.

The bedroom, I could feel it, was where Shirley had been

murdered. In keeping with the killer's modus operandi she, too, had been strangled, her hands and feet had been bound and a plastic bag placed over her head. BTK had locked Shirley's three young children in the adjoining bathroom and had given them some of their toys to play with.

'I feel this murder was opportunistic. He had planned to kill someone else, but that person was out.'

BTK had, in fact, broken into a house nearby and waited for his intended victim but she didn't return home. His craving to murder was such that he had to find someone to kill – Shirley Vian was unlucky.

Eight months after murdering Shirley Vian, BTK had struck again. His seventh victim, Nancy Fox, was murdered in December 1977. Nancy's death hit me the hardest of all – she and I struck up an instant spiritual rapport and could have been great friends had our paths ever crossed on the earth plane. She was kind and sweet-natured.

I'd felt this way about Nancy from the moment Bernie first told me about her – back in the steak diner. From the very start I'd felt this huge warmth for her. Bernie told me BTK persuaded her he was going to rape, not kill, her. Nancy was so trusting she let him bind her and even told him, 'Let's get this over with.' She never stood a chance and my heart went out to her.

Nancy Fox was only twenty-five years old when her life

came to an end. Happy and content in her world, bubbly and characterful, she was also a hard worker holding down two jobs.

We visited Nancy's former home at 843 South Pershing on the following day. Here, we couldn't get access to the house, so I had to work outside the building. She'd been a single girl and living in something akin to a bedsit – a condo as they are known in US.

Again, I was seeing in my mind the events that had taken place and empathizing with the emotions – acute fear was the overriding feeling.

'I think this window was smashed,' I said, pointing to one at back of the building. 'I can hear the sound of breaking glass.'

This, Bernie told us, was where BTK gained entrance. Then I remarked on some mud on the carpet and suggested the killer knocked over a plant. Bernie said there was a plant pot and the police deduced, because the soil had been disturbed, that it had been knocked over.

We continued – the camera was rolling, the mic wired for sound and I was in my dreamworld. Then I talked:

'Nancy is really looking forward to Christmas, she's already decorated her tree and bought presents. She is feeling very happy when she comes into the house. Then BTK jumps out of the cupboard and she becomes fearful. She is scared but she goes along with him.

'BTK had seen Nancy and deliberately planned her death. He picked Nancy out in the jewellery shop where she worked; he went there and he watched her.

'He lets her believe he wants sex with her but that's a lie; it is killing that satisfies his lust, he wants to kill her. He tells her he needs to tie her up and she plays along with him, she's thinking he wants to rape her and if she lets him it will be over. He gags her. She's helpless and she is terrified.'

There was something new, too. I said:

'I feel strongly that BTK wanted anal sex with Nancy Fox.'

Mark, dismissed this idea, instantly. Everyone said I was talking rubbish. BTK, they assured me, had never wanted to have penetrative sex with any of his victims. He was a sexual fantasist who had masturbated after killing some of his victims and that was it. Nevertheless, I stood by what I said – I can only tell it as I see it and my convictions proved to be true as more solid information came to light in the course of the investigation. After I'd got back to the UK this was confirmed in a letter that BTK wrote to the police where he said that he had wanted anal sex with Nancy Fox, and said he would have it with another victim. This was Anna Williams, who, as you'll soon see had a narrow escape.

I also saw something which had never been made public, though the police were aware of it: BTK had stolen a wrapped Christmas present from beneath the tree at Nancy's house and I could also see that it was a doll.

This was confirmed by Bernie in December 2004 after another one of BTK's drops. A doll had been among some of Nancy's personal items found in a park. These were trophies stolen by BTK from the crime scene and left where they would be found and handed in to the police: one of the methods by which he liked to show off his cleverness and bait police investigators. BTK had drawn pubic hair on the half-naked doll. He had also tied its hands behind its back and wrapped a pair of tights around its neck – as he'd done to Nancy.

The hot and cold sensations were, as they had been at the other murder scenes, also present and recognizable to me here: as usual, BTK had turned up the heating and, when they first arrived to investigate, detectives found a cold tap running. Creating a hot atmosphere and ensuring he had very cold hands were an intrinsic and consistent element of this killer's method. With every victim we studied, my hands, too, felt numb with cold and it continually struck me as one of the most tormenting aspects of his method in every case.

BTK wrote a poem called *Oh! Death to Nancy* which opens:

> *What is taht [sic] I can see,*
> *Cold icy hands taking hold of me,*
> *For Death has come, you all can see.*

He sent the poem to Wichita police in 1978 along with a letter claiming responsibility for the murders of both Nancy Fox and Shirley Vian.

During my time in Wichita, I had the good fortune to meet Nancy's stepmother and her father, Dale, who asked me to do a reading for him. Most of what came through was about Dale and a problem with one of his legs, but I had just told him about some jewellery BTK stole from her bedsit when Nancy came through, briefly, which was wonderful for Dale. Nancy sent love to her father and I told him she was at peace, and this gave him great comfort. I wished she had said more, but it just didn't work out.

On my last day in the US we all had lunch together. Dale and his wife gave me lots of presents – souvenirs from Kansas – to take home for my family. They are beautiful, dignified people who really impressed me, just as Nancy did. In fact, alongside Bernie they were the nicest and most decent people I had the pleasure to meet in Wichita. They thanked me for everything I'd done and said they would never give up hope that Nancy's killer would be caught. I wished I could have done more.

It was still day four in Wichita and, since our second day here niggling doubts had been growing in my mind about how the documentary was going to turn out. I had become suspicious because the scenes and sites were all being filmed twice. For example, the scene at the telephone kiosk which BTK used to report the death of Nancy Fox to police: they shot a long scene featuring just the kiosk, and I wasn't included; then they shot a shorter film at the same location with me being interviewed. My instincts told me something was wrong and I felt very edgy about it. Jules had set it up, so I decided to talk it through with her:

'I've got a feeling that this documentary is nothing to do with me. I don't know why, but I've been getting these feelings since my second day here. Why do I feel there is something funny going on?'

I expressed the same concerns to Judith, my PA, but she couldn't shed any light. I made it very clear to Jules that I strongly suspected something fishy was going on but she figured I was safe:

'Don't be so stupid. You've signed a contract. Everything will be fine.'

All I could do was hope that Jules was right and carry on working with the crew. I never asked them the reason they were filming like that – I was afraid I'd look a fool, so I decided to go along with things their way.

When we pulled up at 615 South Pinecrest I knew, immediately, that this was where BTK had planned to kill, but he had not done so. I said:

'I can tell you straight away that no one was murdered

here. But I feel that the small light in the basement was broken when BTK broke in. I feel that BTK sat waiting for someone and they never came home.'

I was right, that evening in April 1979 Anna Williams had been out square dancing and didn't return home until eleven o'clock the next day. It was only when BTK sent a package containing a scarf he had taken from the house, a verse entitled *Oh, Anna Why Didn't You Appear* and a drawing showing her trussed, gagged and bound that she realized how lucky she was to be alive. Terrified, Williams left town.

There was very little to go on at the South Pinecrest house because, apart from the theft of Anna's scarf, no crime had been committed. I did not pick up any feelings, either, at the empty plot where twenty-year-old Kathryn Bright's house once stood. Bright, BTK's fifth victim, was murdered in April 1974.

The ninth victim was Vicki Wegerle, strangled in her home in September 1986 – though she was, in fact, still alive when the killer fled but died later as a result of the strangulation. Here I sensed that BTK had been rushed:

'I can glimpse him peeping out the window. The blind should be up a little bit where he looked out. Something disturbed him. I also feel that he and Vicki's husband may have driven past each other as her husband returned home that day.'

Wegerle's murder remained unsolved until, in a letter received in March 2004, BTK claimed responsibility. The emergency services had moved Vicki's body before detectives reached the scene and as BTK had been forced to flee the evidence in this case didn't bear his familiar trademarks. Sadly, Vicki's husband numbered among earlier suspects.

Apart from White Cloud, I had never encountered an American Indian, so I was really chuffed to be meeting one now. His name was Harry Pryke, he was a forensic artist who worked for the FBI, and as part of the documentary we would build a photofit image of BTK together. A charming man in his fifties, long hair tied back in a ponytail and with a warm smile, Harry was such a joy to work with.

I sat next to Harry and, as I passed on every detail Jagna described, he put it all together on computer. Jagna is a stickler for detail so I knew we would achieve an accurate representation. Her words flashed through my head nineteen to the dozen:

'The eyes need to be wider. The nose should be fatter. The ears are too small. His parting should be over more to the side and he needs more hair, a bushier moustache and fuller cheeks.'

Harry was brilliant and patiently made all the changes Jagna indicated. Interestingly, although this was 2004, Jagna's description was of BTK as he would have looked in the 1970s and 1980s: the years during which he was killing. Then, using high tech age progression techniques Harry added thirty years to the image to bring it up to date. Before I left to return to the UK, I gave a copy to the police.

In retrospect, the photofit turned out to be pretty close. He wasn't a bad looking guy; he just looked so normal.

Harry said he'd 'never forget what a great experience this has been,' then this warm-hearted man gave me a bunch of presents, including an FBI badge and an Indian art calendar. His own art featured in the calendar which he inscribed, 'Great medicine to a great medicine man' – a humbling indication of his respect for me.

That calendar meant so much to me but sadly it was destroyed, along with some other treasured mementos from Wichita, in a fire at my home. The fire happened as I was reading through some of the work for this book.

While I was in Wichita I also drew BTK's signature, the one he used to sign off his letters to the media. Jagna guided my hand as she spoke and the strange configuration and shapes of the letters surprised me. That the killer called himself BTK was, of course, common knowledge but the detail Jagna supplied was hitherto kept under wraps by the police, in order to eliminate hoaxers. The letters' configuration was sexually suggestive by 'stacking' the B, T and K from top to bottom with the B shaped to look like a woman's breasts.

I am a very homely kind of guy, I always have been, so there were inevitably occasions in Wichita when it all became too much for me. Working on the murders was intense and sometimes overwhelming. Bearing in mind I'd rarely set foot outside Cambridgeshire, in Wichita I felt like a fish out of water, so the great kindness shown me by Bernie, Dale and now Harry cheered me up no end when I felt homesick. The staff at the hotel were great, too.

I would sit in my hotel room at night with all sorts of scary thoughts flashing through my mind. I'm telling you, it went into overdrive on occasion. Would BTK be after me? Had he seen me on network TV? Had he read about me in the Wichita press? Did he feel threatened by my presence? Would he try to stop me passing on messages from the spirit world?

The film crew and I had been getting quite a bit of media coverage. Mark had approached Kake-TV – an ABC affiliate – about using some of their BTK archive material and that had spiked their interest. Kake sent a reporter, Theresa Freed, and a cameraman to film some footage of me for the channel. Theresa and I got on like a house on fire. The first time I met her, I told her something extremely personal and she was knocked out by it; it sealed our friendship.

Kake-TV filmed me at all the murder scenes, except the Otero house, recording my feelings about BTK. A local newspaper, the *Wichita Eagle*, ran a story and featured a picture of me taken with one of their reporters. News about the documentary and my part in it was 'out there'. Believe me, I could empathize with the fear held by everyone else in town because I was feeling it too. Did he want to kill me? I was spooked out by BTK.

I was on my bed one night watching TV when there was a knock on my door. I peered through the peephole and saw this strange looking guy with a shock of hair and a huge beard and moustache. 'Ooooh my God, who is he?' I thought – it turned out he was the maintenance man and I felt ridiculous for completely overreacting. But that's how the fear got to you in Wichita back then. People were on edge; and I was one scared psychic.

Now, let me tell you a story. The hotel we stayed at in Wichita boasted 1920s elegance, comfort, great service, great food and a ghost.

One day, I came out of the lift on the seventh floor and saw a man standing at the end of the corridor. He looked like a gangster. In fact, he could have come straight out of *Bugsy Malone*. He was all spruced up in his sharp, pinstripe suit and trilby hat along with a pair of eye-catchingly spivvy shoes.

Vivid as he was – you felt you could reach out and touch him – I knew instantly that he was a ghost.

Keen to find out more I went straight to the desk in the lobby and spoke to one of the receptionists:

'Hey, I've just seen this ghost who looks like a twenties' gangster. He's wearing all the gear; he's got the hat and shoes and everything. What's the story?'

The receptionist burst out laughing and said:

'Oh, you've met him too, have you? He's our resident ghost.'

Apparently he killed his wife, or it might have been his girlfriend, in the hotel, and then killed himself.

We had been in Wichita for almost two weeks and before returning home sweet home I wanted to leave a dossier of the work I'd done with the local police. I went with the documentary team to meet the head of police, and I presented her with a file of my findings which included the two photofits (1970s and 2004 versions), BTK's signature and a psychological profile of BTK.

My profile of him described an ordinary guy who lived with an unsuspecting family, who worked as a maintenance man or as some type of door to door salesman – work that involved visiting people's homes. It described him as crafty and stated that he was able to alter the modus operandi of his murders. I also stated that he would never kill again.

The profile I presented was not what the police were expecting: they were still more inclined to believe that BTK was some kind of sociopath or psychopath who'd been locked away in prison or in a mental institution. This helped explain why no one heard from him for years at a time. 'No,' I insisted. 'This is a man who is really ordinary and if you dropped your shopping, he would not only pick it up but would also carry it home for you.'

I had the feeling as I talked to them that the general consensus amongst the Wichita police was that I was a bit of a fruit loop. I told them, also, that BTK was known to police, but not for violence. I felt his job brought him in contact with them now, but that this was not the case at the time of the killings.

Though detectives listened with interest, my comments, nevertheless, were dismissed and I could say no more to convince the Wichita force that the information I was offering was of value. I left, hoping that time would prove me right.

The police thanked me, saying they were always glad of any help at all on this case – since May 2004 they had been sifting literally thousands of tips via the dedicated e-mail, post office box and tip line they had set up, plus forensics and much else.

I wished them good luck and said, 'I really hope it won't be too long before you catch him. Just remember what I said about him and what you are up against.'

When the day came to return home I was hugely relieved. I didn't mind returning to damp October mornings and grey skies – that is England – and I had missed my family. As I packed my bags, only one thought was in my mind, 'I can't wait to get back home.'

Back in England, I couldn't get the BTK case out of my mind. Though nothing would ever match the intensity of my experiences at Soham, this felt like the most major thing I'd ever been involved in. It was such a big deal in the States, and had been for over thirty years – it had affected so many lives and to see the hold it still had on people over there was mindblowing. ABC TV and KAKE-TV invited me back for interviews but I'd had enough of Wichita; I gave them a couple of phone interviews and that was it. How extraordinary it had all been, I thought as I relived everything I'd been through in the past two weeks. And the flashbacks into BTK's soul were still with me. They lasted only fleetingly, a couple of minutes or so, and they reminded me that BTK walked free and the people of Wichita would not sleep until he was caught. Though Jagna had told me that BTK would never kill again, I knew that nobody there would feel safe until he was behind bars, and who could blame them? No one I spoke to back home had heard of BTK.

I'd been home for a week or so when I typed the letters

BTK into *Google*. Among various relevant websites, I came across one based in the US run by a guy called Tom Voigt and dedicated solely to BTK and news up-dates. The site had a chat room – I had never 'entered' one before and when I typed in my name I was flooded with responses from people who thought I was a hoaxer. I'd had no clue my name was so recognizable in connection with BTK.

I tried to convince them to no avail, and so it went on until Tom Voigt came online and suggested I phone him at home. It was well past midnight here in England but I called and that was all the proof he needed. He was very excited:

'My God, this is incredible, speaking to you is amazing. I wonder if I could ask you to come on our website a few hours a week and talk on the chat room?'

My experiences and spiritual encounters would be just what people were looking for, Tom told me. He said the site was getting three million hits a day and people were desperate for any information they could get on BTK. It was also monitored by the police in case of fresh leads. So I agreed, I said, 'I'd love to'. I couldn't believe how closely they were following the case, and the excitement that could be caused amongst them at even the smallest hint of a new development. I remember one day, before Rader was arrested, the chat room users thought BTK was online with them and it caused mass hysteria. 'Oh he's here, he's listening, will he trace us? Will he find us?' But it wasn't him. My clairsentience had told me not to get too excited about it, that they were barking up the wrong tree.

No longer homesick or stressed, I could work more closely with the spirits and I therefore began to pick up much more precise information about BTK. My best work on him came out on the BTK chat room.

The morning after I'd spoken to Tom I went back on the website and started leaving messages. Jagna told me what to say, and I told them what she told me. I described that a drop would be made that night – December 14. A package would be left in a park by BTK and I could see a doll in it and the doll would be bound and I felt it was meant to be Josephine Otero. And, sure enough, that's what happened.

I also said that the drop would include some jewellery and a hair clip that had belonged to Josephine. I called the hair clip a 'bobby', even though I didn't know what a bobby was until the Americans informed me it's what they call a hair clip – I just say the words as they come to me. Although nothing has been said publicly about this event, I feel it is true.

I forecast two further drops that BTK would make to police and the media which did prove correct:

'You can bet on it that one of those drops will lead to

BTK being traced. It will be his undoing. It will happen within a week,' I typed into the chat room. 'In fact, BTK will be caught by a slip up of his own doing, through a mistake he makes on the computer.'

BTK was finally captured by police after sending in information on a floppy disk made on his church computer where he was a respected and senior member of the community. It was traced right back to the church. The mistake BTK made was to leave information on the disk that could be traced back to him.

Jagna also told me when BTK would be caught:

'It will be in 2005, probably in February, Dennis,' was the message she gave me. And Dennis Rader (BTK) was arrested on 25 February 2005.

I gained more information about BTK's job of work, too, and posted on the website that he drove a blue van with a distinctive sun logo on it. Jagna had described it thus:

'It looks like the way a kid would draw the sunshine. The logo is like a circle made up of triangles, that is how I see it.'

Rader had worked for a security firm called ADT for fourteen years in the 1970s and 80s, the period during which he was murdering most actively, and the logo Jagna described matched the one ADT then had on their vans. At the time of his arrest, Rader was working as a compliance supervisor at Park City in Wichita. The contact with the police through his job – discussed in the profile I'd given detectives in Wichita – was because he would have to liaise with them during the course of his work.

I told the chat room I could see a connection with dogs and it transpired Rader's job at Park City included checking that dogs in the neighbourhood were kept under control. Jagna told me about BTK's house: that it had no front porch – unusual, as the majority of houses in Wichita have front porches – that it was white and there was a shed set back from the road plus a detached garage. Rader's house matches exactly this description; the shed was where he hid his 'trophies', the personal items stolen from each of his victims. I said BTK was aged between fifty-five and sixty-five – Rader was fifty-nine years of age at the time of his arrest.

I always said that Nancy Fox was BTK's favourite, she was his joy, his prize killing. At the time I didn't understand why, but when Radar confessed, we learned that Nancy was indeed a favourite because she had cooperated with him. He admitted this, and that he'd observed her at her work at Wichita Mall where she was always so courteous to customers at the jewellery shop.

I told about the kit that BTK carried with him, containing the tools he used for his savage killings – the plastic bags, the tapes and bindings.

None of this information that I had posted on the website

came into the public domain until after Rader had been arrested.

Once I was back in the UK and had begun to get involved with the BTK website, Jagna told me about the deaths of two other women which police had yet to connect with BTK, and both murders were, at that time, unsolved. Jagna told me their names: Marine Hedge and Dolores Davis. At first, everyone laughed when I told them BTK was also responsible for the murders of Hedge (aged fifty-three), who was killed in April 1985, and Davis (aged sixty-two), his last known victim who was bound and strangled in January 1991. These women were older than BTK's former 'projects', as he called them, so the police did not make the connection to him. But the killer had changed tack to avoid detection; he was one very cunning monster.

I had the last laugh, as it were, when BTK confessed to killing both women, though in the circumstances it was a very hollow victory.

Strangely enough, I could see that BTK liked the numbers 3 and 5. He stalked his victims and knew their house number. It was no coincidence that the Oteros' house number was 803, Kathryn Bright's was 3217, Shirley Vian's was 1311, Nancy Fox's was 843 and Marine Hedge's was 6254. There seemed no rhyme or reason for how BTK picked his victims, but he certainly liked those numbers.

In numerology the number 3 is for self-expression – and

these killings were the most blatant way for him to express his perversion. The number 5 is the freedom number and represents the 'all or nothing'. There was no half-way with BTK: when he went into those houses to kill, that's exactly what he did. He never listened to any pleas from his terrified victims.

The Wichita police monitored the BTK chat room and followed up everything I posted on it. News of my involvement on the BTK case spread to home shores even before Radar's arrest and subsequent confession, with headlines in national newspapers like the *Daily* Star about my work.

Dennis Rader, would never again bind, torture and kill.

And the documentary? A couple of weeks after I returned home, I was informed that the documentary would not include me when it was broadcast. I was very disappointed.

One of my biggest disappointments about the BTK case was that I had failed to figure out why Jagna kept telling me, 'He's like you Dennis, he's like you.' Throughout my time in Wichita she kept repeating those words and I kept asking for clues, clutching at straws, but she never told me the answer. It infuriated me and niggled away at me.

After BTK's arrest it clicked: Dennis, of course. That's what Jagna was trying to tell me, but I didn't know how to interpret what she was saying. Why couldn't she just say straight out, 'His name is Dennis'? That would have been so much simpler, but it doesn't always work that way.

I was horrified to learn that BTK's name was Dennis but, I promise, that is all we have in common.

Limerick:
the Not-so-lucky Irish

Ireland's top chat show host, Pat Kenny, was about to interview me on RTÉ's (Radio Telefís Éireann) *The Late Late
Show*. Kenny pulls no punches and I was expecting a grilling.
The slick, veteran broadcaster would, I imagined, take a
sceptical line on psychics – he certainly wouldn't be the first
– and treat my work with scorn.

There are sceptics, of course, and I don't mind – everyone
is entitled to their own opinion. I've faced enough TV and
radio audiences to know I can stand my ground and get
my point across, but still, in Dublin that Friday night in
January 2007 I was apprehensive. Billed as the 'psychic
detective' I was about to step under the spotlight on the
country's most popular and prestigious TV show.

Pat Kenny's introduction took me by surprise because
he gave me a great build up:

'They claim that they can talk to the dead. They say that they can prove there is an afterlife and deliver messages to the bereaved from beyond the grave. A load of hocus-pocus? I'd certainly need some convincing.

'But I was taken aback when Holly Wells's father [interviewed on the show in March 2005] told me about a psychic who was a tremendous help in solving the murder of his daughter. That psychic not only worked on the Holly Wells case, but also helped catch a serial killer who was on the run for thirty-one years. Most recently, he has been to Ireland to help on the cases of the Irish missing women.'

Now feeling safer in the hot seat, I began to relax and took charge by passing on a message to my inquisitor:

'I thought you would like to know that I had a text message from Kevin Wells today and he asked me to send his regards to you and your family.'

We spoke about the Holly Wells case and the BTK serial killer. Then, more topically, about the Irish missing women. In the Irish republic during the 1990s at least six young women vanished mysteriously. The cases remain unsolved to this day and police hold out little hope of finding any of the women alive. I had made several visits to Ireland in the course of helping two of the families to try and trace their daughters: Fiona Pender, aged twenty-five and a former model, was seven months pregnant when she was last seen by her mother in Tullamore, County Offaly, in August 1996; and another girl who went missing at the age of eighteen. Though her parents contacted me to ask for my help, I know they are private people so I won't identify her or her family. In the case of Fiona Pender, I have given a name to police.

My slot on the show went well. Pat gave me free rein to talk and I grabbed it; the audience was riveted and I was so chuffed. What's more, the guest line up that night included Britt Ekland – who I used to have a crush on. Not only was I on air for almost twice as long as my famous idol but she also gave me a kiss!

In terms of raising my profile, the *The Late Late Show* did me a huge favour, sparking off a flood of calls from people wanting to speak to me and keen to book readings. It also opened many new doors for me in Ireland and I now work in Cork, Kerry, Wexford, Waterford, Galway, Dublin and, most importantly, Limerick.

For me, Limerick would mean gangland killings and grieving families.

Three hundred miles away in Limerick, a heartbroken mother sat crying, hanging on my every word as I told Pat Kenny about my work with families of the disappeared. Mary Kelly was listening and seeing in me her only chance of discovering what had happened to her youngest son, seventeen-year-old Richard, who had been missing for eleven months.

The gardaí had had little information to offer her and, frantic with worry, she had spent hours searching the streets and putting up homemade posters showing Richard's cheeky, freckled face. She yearned to have him home.

After almost a year with no news Mary was feeling very much alone but she refused to give up on finding any answers and she continued to hope that Richard would walk back into the house and ask for his favourite cheese on toast sandwich.

After Mary had seen me on TV she was straight on the phone to her ma and her friends, wanting to know if they had seen the show – wanting to tell them she had seen a chance of finding Richard. And thus Mary was the reason I made the first of many unforgettable visits to Limerick.

The great seaport of Limerick on Ireland's western shores stands on the banks of the mighty River Shannon. It is the third largest city in the Irish republic and boasts a rich history dating back to the Viking era. Within its bounds, however, is Moyross, the sprawling housing estate largely responsible for winning Limerick the unattractive moniker of Stab City.

Moyross is on the city's north side while the smaller but equally grim Southill is on the south side – and that's where Mary lives. Moyross and Southill breathe dereliction – high unemployment, drug-fuelled gangland wars, torched properties, shootings, stabbings, theft. Despite being virtually penniless, Mary determined she would see me. She had been to England only once in her life but she was ready to go again. She wasted no time in calling my PA, Judith, and pleading for an appointment:

'I've got to see Dennis McKenzie. I don't care how much it costs – I'll borrow the money to get there.'

Judith couldn't fail to hear the distress in Mary's voice and, moved by her wavering words and tears, spoke to me about how I might fit her in then reported back to Mary:

'I've had a word with Dennis and he will see you in two months' time, in Dublin. That will be sooner than his first free appointment in England. He can see you at the end of his readings, I have booked you in for nine o'clock in the evening.'

The reading would take place at my hotel in Dublin's Finglass district. Mary couldn't thank Judith enough.

I didn't know it when I first read for her, but I was the fourth psychic Mary had seen in the hope of finding some clue to Richard's whereabouts. The first had told her there was too much blackness around her and she would have to 'wait for the wall to go down' before having a proper reading. I thought that sounded like a load of rubbish, but the psychic had at least been decent enough not to charge anything for it. Some psychics use auras and see colours around their clients but I don't work that way.

Then Mary saw a white witch, and the first thing she

asked her for was money. Again, it was a waste of time as she didn't tell Mary anything different from what she could have read in the newspapers. As Mary sobbed, the white witch told her to stop crying, and that she could look forward to being reunited with her missing son within six days.

Mary was ecstatic, believing she could plan one helluva party to celebrate Richard's homecoming. She clung to that hope for every minute of the following week: she waited for the phone to ring and waited to see him walk through the front door. But, of course, nothing happened. That's a good example of what I mean when I say there are so many charlatans about who just tell people what they want to hear and have no guilt about taking their money.

The third psychic she went to also told Mary there was too much blackness around her, but she'd just picked up on emotional distress which she saw as being cloaked in darkness. All she could tell was that she saw Richard in prison and to come back if the blackness lifted. Mary had wasted a fortune.

While she may have been short of money, Mary Kelly is certainly not short of friends and a whip-round raised enough to hire transport to see me in Dublin – and enough for Mary to travel with her cousin Noreen and Aunt Mary plus friends Lorraine, Patrick and Willy.

This was my first return visit to Dublin since my TV appearance two months earlier. On the evening of her appointment – 18 March, Mothering Sunday – Mary walked in nervously and alone. For me, it was just another reading, a normal reading – if you can have such a thing. She sat facing me and her tired eyes looked anxiously at me. She fidgeted with her hands on the table as I introduced myself and explained how our session would unfold. Mary bit her lip, looked down at her hands and nodded, keen for me to proceed. She looked drained; I could see that the last weeks had been hard for her, but as yet I knew nothing of her problem.

'OK, love?' I asked, trying to make her feel at ease.

I asked her for her date of birth and as soon as I started doing her numerology I picked up worries about a child. My feelings were telling me she was very, very troubled.

'I can feel that you are worried about a child. I can see a child is lost.'

Her son had come through to me; snapshots of his face came through to me. The moment I saw her boy in the spirit world I knew that he was dead. I could see his cropped fair hair and a huge grin on his freckled face. He spoke in a broad Irish accent. The youngest of Mary's three sons was surely the apple of his mother's eye, and he was goodhearted. I could also smell him – he came through stinking like a brothel of the aftershave he was overfond of.

'I've got your son here, and he's so happy, why is he so happy?' I asked her.

'No one calls him "Richard", they call him "Happy",' Mary said. 'He got the name from his father, only his father never deserved it – but my boy did, he always had a cheery smile on his face.'

Then she told me that her son was missing, and I prepared to tell her the news she dreaded most.

'He's not missing, he's not lost,' I began.

'That's it, he's over in England after all,' she replied quickly, her face lighting up.

Happy's mother was grasping at straws. I felt that familiar gnawing in my stomach and my mouth dried up as I reached out, took hold of her hand and said:

'Sweetheart, you'll never see your son on this plane again. Your boy has been murdered.'

Mary broke down in tears and I tried to comfort her. I hugged her and held her tight and wished my message to her could have been different.

Naturally the boy's mother was desperate to know what had happened to him. I'd seen his killers' vicious attack on him and I'd felt a sharp pain on the side of my head. Happy's spirit was telling me that someone had smashed his head in with a concrete slab, and so this was what I had to tell his mother. When Mary heard the three names Happy had given me, she nearly fell over and exclaimed:

'One of those people you have named was with my Happy at the house on the last day of his life. How can that be?'

Then I went on to talk about two cars, one red, one white – which she recognized – telling her that one of the cars was the reason her son had been killed. Happy told me he had stolen the white car during the last weekend he was alive and Mary confirmed that he had been driving a white one on the day he disappeared. The message I'd received told me that his life had ended in the early hours of Sunday morning, sometime after 4am, and also that the red car had been stolen specifically for the purpose of murdering Happy. It was later found abandoned and burnt out.

Happy told me some personal things about his life which I passed on, and he spoke about the fact he'd been a joyrider and car thief and the trouble he'd been in with the gardaí. I could see the gardaí searching for him when he was hiding under the table at his aunty's house, 'They didn't find him, did they?' I said to Mary.

As Mary told me about Happy and their life at home, my heart went out to her. Would she like me to work on the case? 'Yes,' she'd love that – but, 'I can't afford it,' she said. 'Don't you worry about that, my love,' I told her. 'Because this won't cost you a brass farthing.'

I have never charged anyone when working on a murder

case. How can you make money from that? You can't. It would be crass. I wouldn't do it, regardless of whether they could afford it or not.

I would soon be making my first trip to Stab City.

I saw Mary again five months later, in August 2007. I was back in Ireland, but this time in the beautiful west-coast town of Ballybunnion in County Kerry, where I was fully booked again for readings.

She brought her mother, Rita, along, a lovely, warm lady. While they were waiting for me, the manageress of the hotel asked to see Happy's photo and, as they turned it over, a white butterfly appeared on Rita's hand. Rita was so excited about it:

'Dennis, I know it's a good sign,' she told me and I agreed that it was.

She was as keen as Mary was to find Happy's body and give him a decent burial:

'Please find my grandson before I pass my last breath. Please,' she pleaded.

Her words touched me deeply and I promised that 'by hook or by crook' I would do everything I could – and I meant it.

Whilst we were sitting there talking with each other, Happy came through with a message which surprised both women:

'I'm getting that there is a bracelet missing. Happy is with me and is telling me it's no longer with him. I think Lisa has got it. I think she's got that bracelet.'

Mary confirmed that she had bought Happy a special bracelet one Christmas and that her son had known a girl called Lisa who lived in their neighbourhood. I can't say for definite whether the bracelet has ever been in Lisa's possession, but that is definitely what Happy's spirit told me.

Mary and Rita spread out some local maps on the table. I had a strong feeling about where we needed to go and kept describing an area outside Limerick, but I couldn't pinpoint it on the map. I felt I was going around in circles.

'This is no good,' I said. 'It's not working this way. I'm back here in November; I'll come and see you in Limerick and we'll take it from there. We'll go out and see what we can find.'

The two women were over the moon. Mary had been alone on her mission, trudging the streets posting up pictures of her son. I hoped the very least I would do was help find Happy's remains and make his grandmother's wish come true.

Happy had faced problems throughout his life. He suffered from ADHD (attention deficit hyperactivity disorder) and, as a result, by the time he'd reached eleven, no school could handle his disruptive behaviour. From then on he'd occasionally be made to sign up to one type of course or another but he never lasted long on these; it was pretty clear his mind was always on other things.

He'd nicked lots of cars and was a habitual joyrider and was, therefore, well known to the local gardaí. I'm not defending what he did, but he was a lad with a good heart who'd grown up on an estate where pretty much all the influences were bad, and that had a lot to do with the trouble he made. Happy had not been given any education or training which could have helped him do something useful with his life.

I felt sorry for the boy because he'd been deprived of any chance to break the vicious cycle of poverty and criminality he was born into.

Happy's spirit had told me about the rough time he had with the Limerick gardaí. Policing Limerick must be difficult, I don't doubt – not for nothing did it get its nickname. In the past eleven years there have been 127 mostly gang-related killings in Limerick – including Happy's – but just fourteen convictions, and in 2008 Limerick tipped the statistical scales as Europe's murder capital.

I have just come back from Waterford where I read in the newspapers about a boy shot recently in Limerick. This time, in a case of mistaken identity, it is a boy from a middle-class family who has been killed, not one of the lads from the Southill estate. The gardaí are pulling out all the stops and the whole Republic is in a furore about Limerick's gangland killings. As a result, the Irish government is putting millions of euros into getting more gardaí on the streets of Limerick.

Mary Kelly didn't approve of her son's way of life, but she was always there for him whenever he got into trouble. Sometimes he'd get arrested and phone her and say, 'Mam, I'm in the barracks.' And she would go to get him out. One thing about Happy was that he always turned up in court on time; he never failed to appear. Another thing about him was that he was meticulous about his appearance – at twelve o'clock everyday he would get up, have a shower and get dressed.

The boy's account of his life and its brutal end brought tears to my eyes. He and his mates nicked cars because that's what you did where they lived. Happy had nicked a car and now he was dead but, as far as I was concerned, his mother adored him and I would do whatever I could to help.

As Happy left his home for the last time on Sunday 24 April 2006, he called out a cheerful goodbye to his mum as he closed the door behind him:

'Bye, Ma, I love you.'

'Love you too, son. And you be careful now. I don't want

you getting into any trouble,' she called back, and busied herself in the kitchen.

Happy was under a police curfew for some car stealing offences and had to be home by ten o'clock each evening:

'Happy knew he had to be home by ten and he was very good about coming back by curfew. There were times when I would walk the roads looking for him, but he would come in,' Mary told me.

But that last night was different. Happy had phoned home:

'Mam, can I go down the road babysitting with my girl-friend?' he'd asked.

Mary was concerned about him breaking his curfew, but agreed:

'Yes. But coming back up, you be careful so the gardaí don't see you breaking your curfew. I want you to get a taxi home.'

That was the last time they spoke. When Mary went to bed that night, her son had not come home. She thought he might have decided to stay the night at the house where he was babysitting and she was wishing she hadn't agreed that he could go.

'I thought if I phoned him, he would go and take a car to get back home, so I decided against it,' she said.

At three o' clock in morning, Mary woke up with a jolt. A strange feeling came over her as she sensed that something terrible was happening to her son. Her mother's instinct was telling her that something was very wrong. She wanted to phone him, but didn't.

Mary is a devout Catholic and prayed fervently for Happy's safe return. She couldn't go back to sleep and tossed and turned, listening and longing to hear him coming through the door. At six o'clock that morning she went downstairs. Suddenly, she went cold and thought, 'I don't think I'll ever see my child again.'

'I can't explain that feeling to anyone,' she told me. 'But a coldness hit me and that's what I thought. It was terrifying.'

She wept as she recalled that eerie feeling and her terrible premonition.

Flying in to Shannon Airport, I looked down at the patch-work of richly green fields below. The mild, wet climate on Ireland's west coast makes this ideal farming country and being a country boy at heart I always feel a sense of joy when I drive through this lush, rural landscape.

Had I been visiting Limerick as a tourist I might have soaked up some 13th-century history at King John's Castle or taken myself off to the city's fabulous art gallery and museum. But I was here to work and the Limerick I was heading for was certainly not on the tourist trail. It was October – seven months since Mary and I had first met and I had told her that her son had been murdered.

I got a shock when I arrived at Mary's house on O'Malley Park, one of Southill's four residential 'parks' (Moyross has twelve). I've been to some rough areas in my life, and I don't scare easily, but there's no way you would find me walking around there on my own at night. Unemployment in Southill in 1983 was four times above the national average, not surprising as only some fifty per cent of over-sixteens on the estate have had any formal education to speak of.

As I drove into O'Malley Park I was passing burned-out houses with their roofs ripped off, walls covered in graffiti such as 'Scumbag Killers', and doors and windows closed with metal shutters. Then I would come across a spick-and-span house with a wonderfully neat garden and plants lovingly tended. The contrast was surreal.

Fortunately, Mary will soon be living in a brand new house. Two thousand homes in Southill are due to be demolished and rebuilt in an attempt to restore a sense of pride in the local community – there are plenty of good people here who despise the gang culture that dominates.

I had been warned not to go anywhere near Southill – even the gardaí fear these streets. Recently when a garda officer got out of his car and a bullet shot past his ear he jumped straight back in and drove off. I was in the worst ghetto I have ever seen in my life, but I didn't have any fear.

*   *   *

While inside Mary's home everything was clean, cosy and very homely, the outside looked like so many others on the estate: a pebbledash council house, rundown and neglected, with its garden being used as a rubbish dump. There was a shed at the end of the garden:

'That's where Happy kept his horse, Tato,' Mary told me. 'I couldn't keep it after he'd gone. He was great with animals and we got him a horse and he trained it. He would ride out on it in the morning and wouldn't come home until night time. He rode bareback and he'd ride all around the estate.'

At first, I found this really strange. But now I've been to Limerick a few times, I've grown accustomed to seeing lads riding bareback or tearing along in a little horse-drawn cart called a sulky – they look a bit like gladiators. I thought it bizarre how these boys love smart cars yet they love their horses, too.

To understand the Southern Irish working-class horse culture you've got to forget about smart stables and fancy tack and think more along gypsy lines. The city-dwelling horse will be penned in on a patch of grass two yards square and tethered to a stake, and it will be ridden up and down the estate either bareback with a bit of string around it's neck in place of reins, or driven from a sulky. It's the way of life in every working-class town and city in the South. From workhorse to pony to pure-bred racehorse, the horse is an intrinsic part of Irish culture.

I had learned something new, then, and I would learn so much more about the dark side of Ireland.

I arrived at Mary Kelly's house on a Sunday morning and was greeted in her kitchen by a stream of people, young and old, curious to meet this psychic – Mary must have filed more than forty of them in through the front door and then out of the back door. I was introduced to each and every one of them and though they were too many to remember by name, their warm welcome made me feel very special and I shall always remember it. Thanking me over and over again for helping Mary they all hugged and kissed me, shook my hand, slapped me on the back and even cried over me. I was overwhelmed.

Mary's friends and neighbours had never before known of an outsider, such as I was, willing to offer help to 'one of their own', as they put it: 'Thank you so much for coming, you don't know how much this means'; they continued: 'She deserves her Happy back so she can give him a decent burial'; 'That boy was the apple of her eye'.

'Believe me,' I told everyone, 'I will do my best to find Happy's body.'

When everyone left and the house was quiet I sat with Mary in the living room where displayed on the sideboard were photos of Happy – smiling, of course – and his two older brothers, Robert and Edward.

Mary was excited, saying how much she had been looking forward to my coming and emphasizing how desperately she hoped I could find Happy's body. As she spoke, I felt Happy come through:

'I've got Happy with me, Mary. He's come through straight away.'

Tears filled her eyes but she smiled when he said, 'Mum, I want a toasted sandwich.' Then he asked about his horse and told me some personal things about his family.

I was looking for some indication from Happy to show where to search for his body. I asked Mary if I could hold one of his personal possessions – this would give me a stronger connection with his spirit – and she handed me a key on a chain. She couldn't have given me anything better, 'That was Happy's key for nicking cars,' said Mary.

I spread out a map of Limerick and swung the key, like a pendulum, all around the city outskirts. The key came to a stop at a spot some thirty miles north of the city and clairsentience gave me an image of what the location would look like. I pointed to the map, looked at Mary straight in the eye and said, 'This is where we need to go, Mary. Let's go now and find Happy.'

*   *   *

I had pinpointed on the map where we needed to go, but some local knowledge would be useful, so Happy's best friend Martin joined us along with Mary and her brother, Turlough. Judith, my PA, had joined me on this trip and she was behind the wheel.

As we piled into my hire car I noticed a coach parked nearby with about thirty people onboard. Mary's friends had booked a coach so they could join in. It was going to be a day's outing for them, albeit an unusual one. Mary was fine with it; they were friends and family who wanted to be with us on this very important day. It became almost laughable when the bus driver announced, 'Room for one more,' and a woman piped up, 'Great! Let me just get my packed lunch.' Then yet more friends drew up in cars behind the coach, along with a local community gardaí officer in Mary's trust.

In all my years working as a psychic I'd never led a cavalcade of observers – it was a unique experience. I think they were expecting I would roll back a rock and there Happy would be.

We waited for the final passenger to collect her packed lunch and jump on the coach, then we set off. Martin was familiar with the area we were headed for and as we drove into the countryside, he directed us as best he could based on what my feelings were telling me. I was using all my psychic powers to guide me – clairaudience, clairsentience and clairvoyance – as well as having help from Happy's spirit.

During the journey, even more cars joined our cavalcade because everyone there was calling up their friends, 'Come and join us, we're out looking for Happy with Dennis.' When our car took a wrong turning down a narrow country lane we had to make a U-turn, and so did the coach and all the cars behind it – it was so comical to see.

We had been driving for forty minutes when we came to a lay-by:

'We need to stop. I feel something here. Pull over now,' I told Judith.

Martin knew why this location was significant: 'The white car Happy nicked was found over there,' he said, pointing to an area opposite the lay-by.

I pictured the white car in my mind: 'This is odd,' I said. 'It's parked strangely. It wasn't parked by the road, the car has been spun and it's in the middle of the road.'

For some reason, Happy had driven the car to this location where it had been abandoned. But the boy's body was not here, that I knew, and I wanted to move on. At the lay-by, the whole entourage had climbed out of the coach and their cars, wanting to know what was happening, and their presence was proving a real hindrance, so I had no choice but to ask them to let us continue our search without them. Reluctantly, they agreed to return home, and now, with just my car and the gardaí community officer's, I felt much more relaxed.

We continued north, using my psychic abilities almost like a satellite navigation system to follow the route Mary's son had travelled on the last day of his life. After another forty minutes we came to a large, stone bridge – which I had seen before in my mind's eye – and I knew this was the right area. We drove across the bridge and stopped. There was a lorry park on one side of the road and a field on the other. I got out of the car, looked at the crystal clear river flowing under the bridge and, apart from the lorry park, it was picture-postcard perfection. My psychic senses confirmed that we were in the right place and now I must relate what I knew to Mary:

'Mary, this is it. Happy was murdered here. This bridge is where he met his end, but his body's not here, it's within a few miles' radius.'

Martin looked very upset but Mary held her brother's arm and I admired how she kept her composure. I felt sickened by the pictures that flashed into my mind's eye and sickened, too, as I experienced Happy's fear, but I continued:

'What I am seeing is men throwing things. I think they are throwing rocks and concrete slabs at Happy.

'I think there was a meeting by this bridge. I think Happy was meeting the gang here to be given instructions about the other car he had stolen – it belonged to this gang. I feel he met them here late in the evening on the Sunday he went missing. I see the gang pulling up in their cars. Happy pulls up in the white car. I think he drove to this meeting in the white car then, after they'd killed him, one of the gang must have dumped it beside the lay-by.

'Happy was frightened here. He was fearful. I am so sorry, Mary. At first, he thought he was just going to get a thrashing but he soon realized he was in very deep trouble. He thought he could blag his way out of it. He couldn't.'

But where was the boy's body? I felt a weight crushing down on me and pinning me down and found myself saying:

'Wherever he is, he won't be got by hand because there is something holding him down, my love.'

It was a shocking statement to make and I didn't know exactly what it meant, but I felt there was great pressure holding Happy down. We looked at the map; I swung his key over it and it showed we were close. We drove around for a while but then returned to the bridge. The key kept pulling us back to the bridge. And, suddenly, I could hear the boy clearly in my head telling me this was where he wanted us to be and I cried out that I knew for certain his body was very close.

Jagna then came through; she had been chipping away with bits of information throughout, but now she was emphatic and repeating the name 'Brigid' and the words 'dyke' and 'bodyke'. I had no clue what she meant, but

Mary suggested something to do with her grandmother who's name was Bridget, but that was as much as we could deduce.

We took one last look around, then drove on a little further and stopped at another location that I believed also had a strong connection with Happy and the stolen cars. Though it was unclear what this link was, I could sense that something really significant in relation to poor Happy's last few hours occurred here.

By this stage, we were all feeling emotionally drained and very tired, so we called it a day and headed back to Mary's house. She cooked up a delicious supper and her friends fussed over Judith and myself. I had booked a hotel in Ballybunnion which was a good hour and a half's drive and, without thinking, I'd mentioned I was almost too knackered to bother with it. I was so touched when, as soon as I'd said it, Mary and her friends wanted to scrape together their last few euros and book a room each in Limerick for Judith and me. They said they wanted to show their appreciation. We say glibly, 'I'm skint', but we don't know what it's like to be *really* skint, as skint as the people living in Southill. Obviously I didn't accept but I was bowled over by their offer.

As I prepared to take my leave, Mary cried the tears she had been holding back all day. I gave her a hug and promised I was there for her and that we hadn't found all the answers but we were close. Then I told her that I would be returning to Ireland in December but, 'It won't be to look for Happy because he will have been found', I was certain of it.

On 28 November 2007, fishermen found Richard 'Happy' Kelly's badly decomposed remains in Lough Brigid, near Bodyke, in County Clare. Lough Brigid lies sixteen miles north of Limerick and about two miles away from where we had been searching. That's what Jagna had been trying to tell me, but I had not been able to interpret her words. Two concrete slabs had been tied to each of Happy's legs, so that's what was meant by the weight I felt pinning me down. I gave all the information I had gathered to the Killaloe garda (responsible for the Lough Brigid area) and to the Limerick garda.

A recent inquest report described Kelly being murdered after stealing a car belonging to a notorious city criminal gang. Arrests have been made, but no one has yet been charged.

When Mary Kelly was told that her son's body had been found it was, for her, the end of an agonising twenty months: finally, her son would have his funeral. Funnily enough, I knew before Mary did that Happy's body had been found in the lake; I'd heard it from the spirit in question when he hitched a ride in my car.

I like to drive a flashy car, it's my one indulgence. It's a bright yellow sporty Hyundai Coupe with noisy twin exhausts and brilliant acceleration. It's a real head-turner. I was driving it two nights before Happy was found when, suddenly, there were hundreds of pinprick sized twinkling lights darting around in front of my eyes. They were exactly like the ones I had seen in the box room at Janet's parents' house but, this time, I thought them a sign that something special was going to happen, though I couldn't work out what.

Nothing happened until the following night when I was driving up the A1 coming home from a psychic fair. I'd just turned off just past the Stevenage turning and — there was Happy sitting on the front passenger seat. Clearly, he was the reason for the flashing lights – early warning lights, if you like. I'd leaned over to pick up something off the seat, and there he was, looking as real as you or me, nothing transparent or ghostly about him at all. I think he was enjoying the ride in a fast car:

'Hey, nice car, Den,' he said. 'If you were in Ireland with this, I'd nick it and take it for a spin.'

I had to laugh; it was so true to form. I know how much he would have loved to burn rubber around Southill in my car. There was a message he wanted me to pass on to Mary:

'Will you ring Mam up and tell her I'm coming in out of the cold? Tell her I'm coming home and that I love her.'

Happy sat with me for a good couple of minutes and his presence felt quite normal to me – I am accustomed to seeing spirits every day and sometimes they sit in my car. I felt so pleased that Mary's wish to give him a decent burial was soon to come true.

When I phoned Mary first thing the following morning her first words were, 'He's been found, Dennis'; she had heard via the official channel. I passed on Happy's message and told her about the lights that had heralded him turning up in my car and she was so thrilled to hear about it.

Two weeks after his body had been found, Mary was finally able to give her son his funeral. I couldn't be there but she told me later that those twinkling lights had appeared at the church and had given her great comfort:

'All the lights in the church were off and all around there were lights dancing about like you had in your car, Dennis. I really felt Happy was with us,' she told me.

There was a kind of postscript to all this. Happy's friend and fellow joyrider Martin, who'd been so helpful in our search, had a serious car crash before the funeral – he suffered a severe head injury but he's making good progress.

Mary visited him in hospital and Martin surprised her one day when he asked, 'Why, when you go home, does Happy stay here sitting on my bed?' It seemed that Martin was convinced that his old friend was in the room with him and they had been chatting away just like old times; I imagine Happy's spirit wanted to offer Martin some comfort.

Mary was still so scared and distraught that she refused to visit her son's grave unless I was with her, so, two weeks after the funeral, I returned to Limerick. When we arrived at the graveyard and I saw the floral tributes there was one which rendered me speechless – a yellow sports car with grey side-fins; an identical replica of my car. No one in Limerick had seen or could have known about my car:

'Mary, who sent that yellow car?' I asked.

'Martin,' she replied.

When I spoke to Martin he couldn't explain why he'd wanted that particular car and colours sent for his friend's grave. Happy's spirit must have told Martin about my car; after all, it had impressed him.

Mount St Oliver Cemetery in Limerick is home to too many graves of lives cut short through violence, drugs and poverty. Happy's death opened my eyes to a way of life I never knew existed. Most people have no concept of what it means to be that 'hard up' – Mary would struggle sometimes to find the money to put a meal on the table. Funnily enough, Mary gave me a wallet as a thank you present. I'd never carried a wallet in my life but now, thanks to Mary, I have one with me all the time. Her gift from the heart is all the more precious to me because I know she can ill afford it.

★   ★   ★

Dennis McKenzie

After Happy Kelly's body was discovered in Lough Brigid the Irish media picked up on my involvement in the case. An interview I did on Limerick local radio in December 2007 provoked a response from a listener, Jason, whose nephew had been killed. Jason and his sister, Gabrielle – the boy's mother – tracked me down to the hotel in Ballybunnion where I was giving readings.

Gabrielle had never before consulted a medium, however when Jason told her what he'd heard about me she was keen to see me for a reading. I was fully booked, but, persuaded by the urgency in her tone, offered to squeeze in an appointment for her a couple of days hence.

As Gabrielle sat in the hotel waiting her turn for a reading, a young woman in obvious, extreme distress rushed past her – the woman had been told by me that her brother had shot his mother, his father and then himself. Witnessing this woman's reaction immediately before her first ever reading made Gabrielle very nervous. Nevertheless, as soon as she sat down with me, her son, Gareth, came through:

'It's not long ago that you lost him. It's been weeks rather than months,' I told her.

I looked at her tear stained face and felt a huge surge of warmth and sympathy for another mother who had lost a son.

Gareth had been dead for four weeks, shot and killed two months after his twenty-fifth birthday.

I could tell from the pain I was feeling in my head, my left hand and down my left arm that Gareth had been shot in his left side and had then fallen heavily, hitting his head on a hard surface, a pavement I felt.

I was able to tell Gabrielle that Gareth was a lovely person with a beautiful heart and had a contagious laugh and that though his friends were an evil bunch, Gareth was not like them. I passed on a message that he was very sad and wanted to say 'sorry' to his mother.

'There's no need for him to say sorry. I'm sorry to have lost him,' Gabrielle wept.

Gareth told me he was at peace and asked his mum to protect his partner, Claire, and their three children, and gave me a couple of names – names which Gabrielle was already familiar with in connection with her son's death.

On a lighter note, Gareth also had a message for Claire, who was waiting for Gabrielle in the hotel lobby. The message I thought would amuse and comfort Claire and I wanted to tell her in person. I went to find her which, though I had of course never set eyes on her, was no problem as Gareth had described her to me:

'I had to tell you this myself, my love. Gareth wanted to tell you that you look great and he prefers you this way. [In her stress following the shooting Claire had lost a lot of weight.] He also wanted me to tell you that you've still got a lovely arse.'

Claire did laugh at the message. The little, personal messages from the spirit world can bring so much comfort to those grieving their loss.

Gabrielle was seeking information that might help bring her son's killers to book and I've learned by experience that doing a reading on a case such as this is not enough:

'I need to be there,' I explained to Gabrielle. 'To tell you more, I need to be wherever Gareth was. I can work much better that way.' I also explained that, as always under such circumstances, I would be asking no fee for the help I was offering.

We agreed to meet the following month when I'd be back in Limerick for a service which was to be held in honour of the fishermen who found Happy's body and of myself.

Gabrielle lives on St Mary's Park, yet another of Limerick's notorious estates but also one which is looking forward to a programme of regeneration. In the face of violence and corruption, peace loving residents such as Gabrielle learn to keep themselves to themselves in the hope it will not taint their lives. I saw gardaí here patrolling on foot, but they were backed up by officers in a car and, some distance behind the car, I could see armed officers, too. This place scared me.

Gabrielle had lived on the estate for twenty-eight years

– her ten children were born there – getting on with her everyday life; she told me it's none of her business what goes on behind locked doors. And, surrounded by her family and friends, she has no intention of leaving St Mary's:

'Why should I leave the place I've been happy in all my life, just because my son was murdered?'

Gareth, like Happy, had been a horse lover and he, too, used to ride around the estate in a sulky cart with his pony, Beauty. He, Claire and their children lived just a couple of minutes around the block from Gabrielle and he had been shot and died just yards from his home. How horrible for his family, I thought, to be living so close to the place it had happened.

Gabrielle's son had been involved with the gangs on the estate. The night before the shooting, Gareth had visited his mother and told her about a message on his mobile telling him to call somebody who was in prison. He didn't know why, but it later turned out this person had wanted to warn Gareth that someone was planning to shoot him. Gareth didn't have any credit on his phone, so he couldn't call back. That phone call could have saved his life.

Just after ten o'clock on the morning of 8 October 2007 Gareth stepped outside his house to have a cigarette; he didn't smoke around his children especially as one of them, Gareth junior, had asthma. Gareth's brother, David, had called around to see him and had just left. Suddenly, Claire heard a loud bang and thought it was kids letting off fireworks. But she noticed the front door was open and went out to look for her man.

She saw a body lying on the pavement, motionless, and a man standing over it with a gun pointed down at its head. She didn't know that the man on the ground was Gareth. Claire screamed and the killer looked into her face then ran off. She stood, petrified, and then looked down: first, she recognized Gareth's runners and jacket then she saw his face.

Gabrielle had been at Gareth and Claire's visiting her grandchildren and had also heard the bang. When she went into the street to see what was going on she saw Claire and ran to her. Claire was screaming, 'It's Gareth, it's Gareth. He's been shot.'

Claire took off after the gunman and got as far as her house – about twenty metres from the scene – where Gareth's younger brother who was still a teenager stood, also screaming, by the door. Someone she knew stood beside him and Claire shouted at him for his phone. He told her he didn't have one but she knew that was a lie. He was probably too scared of what might happen to him if he helped her by handing it over, she told me later. Claire shouted at the two men to follow the gunman but by then he was long gone.

She ran back to Gabrielle who was cradling her dying son's head on her lap; she was fighting back tears, wanting to be strong for him. Claire knelt by her man's side and wept over him as she gently rubbed his back. Gabrielle stroked his forehead. A crowd of onlookers had gathered and Gabrielle and Claire, willing Gareth not to die, begged anyone to call an ambulance. But within only a few moments, they realized it was too late.

Gareth's children will grow up without any real memory of their father; the baby was six weeks old, Gareth junior was three and the eldest of the boys was five years old when their father died.

On the day we had arranged to visit the locations related to Gareth's murder, Gabrielle, Claire, Gareth's sister Simone and I all met at Gabrielle's house:

'I don't want you to tell me anything. I just want you to place me in the right spot, and I will tell you what I feel,' I told them.

They would take me to Claire's house first. As they led along the street – starkly reminiscent of those around Southill – I sensed inherent fear and shuddered. I was uneasy and, though I couldn't see anyone, I felt that many eyes were fixed upon me and I felt the people behind the eyes knew who I was and the psychic power I held.

The women nodded agreement when I correctly identified the alleged killer's house and then – from the voices in my head and clairsentience – the house where Gabrielle believes the gun that killed Gareth was hidden. At this point a young man walked by. I think he was checking me out, and voices in my head and clairsentience told me clearly that this man had known about the murder in advance but was not the murderer.

We very soon reached Claire's house. To make a good connection with Gareth's spirit I needed a personal item he'd been fond of. Claire handed me a chain with a horse shoe on it which she'd given him for good luck and, as soon as I held it, Gareth came through. He seemed to want to get a few things off his chest and he kicked off with a curtain rail he'd tried to fix but bodged. It's curious how people's spirits can come out with apparently insignificant events; they must simply want closure on them. He also told me about a private discussion he and Claire had had the night before he died and he told me, too, about the phone message he'd received but not followed up.

We then walked the short distance to the spot where Gareth was shot and I recognized it immediately: I became hot and sweaty and Jagna and my clairsentience told me the gunman had stood there. I could see Gareth's lifeless body being held by the two women who loved him most in the world. I saw Gabrielle pleading with him to, 'Stay with us, keep your eyes open. Don't go to sleep. Please don't go to sleep.' But the pain of his wounds was soon over; he did not suffer for long.

I believed Gareth had crossed a gang member, and sensed that many people had been involved in setting up his murder and that many had seen it happen. 'I can see a camper van parked on the other side of the road,' I said, and pointed where I could see a man running from it and down one of the side streets. I was able to name the names of the person I felt was the killer and the other people involved. I gave the alleged killer's nickname, too – Claire suspected the same person. I felt they had been watching from behind a wall on the corner, waiting for Gareth to step outside his house. I saw that when Gareth lit his cigarette, he was beckoned by one of the gunman's associates and was talking to him with no suspicion that the man was luring him to his death.

Standing there, I was thinking how different life was on St Mary's from anything in Cambridgeshire's sleepy villages when out of the blue a car sped past us at about 90 mph and a boy in the car looked straight at me – his fingers pointing like a gun. Oh yes, they knew who I was and why I was there and what my psychic powers might reveal; this was a warning. It sent shivers through me. Then there seemed to be loads of shifty looking people around – watching from their houses, in cars, riding sulkies and following us on foot. I was a marked man and it was one of the few times in my life I have been really frightened.

As always, I passed on to the garda the names of those I gleaned to be connected with Gareth's murder. No one has yet been charged, but I remain very hopeful that the guilty will be brought to justice.

Although Claire's children have lost their father, I was able to show her that his spirit seemed to be watching over them. Before setting out from her house onto the street I'd felt something like unease around my chest and asked, 'Who has had the asthma attack?'

'That would be little Gareth,' Claire told me.

'I think his dad has been here and that he helped his boy,' I said.

I asked, and Claire confirmed that Gareth junior had had an asthma attack a couple of nights before. She kept his nebulizer in the sitting room, but the door (which had always been tricky to open) was (mysteriously) stuck fast and she couldn't open it until, somehow, as she was raking around the house trying to find other medicine, she found it forced open.

'I think that was Gareth's way of helping his little boy when he needed him,' I told Claire. 'That was Gareth's way of helping you both. He knew how worried you were.'

Gabrielle and Claire were extremely grateful for my help. I sometimes think what a huge burden my ability is, but people such as these need me and I always try to be there for them.

One month following my visit there was an arson attempt on Claire's house – a window had been smashed and something thrown inside to set the place on fire. Gabrielle was driving by and saw the flames just in the nick of time to save the building from total destruction, but there was smoke damage throughout. Since the fire, Claire and her children have been living with Gabrielle: there are ten of them in a two-bedroom house.

Following that fearful walk around St Mary's Park I went straight to Happy's thanksgiving service. Mary was waiting for me at her house and we hugged. Once again, the house was packed with friends and relatives. Mary insisted on going to the church in my hire car. I'd never been to a Catholic church before, so I was feeling very nervous about it – and there I was in pride of place in the front pew! Everyone came up and shook my hand and patted me on the back, though I felt I had done very little.

The priest, Father Pat Hogan, was a very tall man with a beard and the fact that he wore jeans under his cassock really tickled me. The service was wonderful and very touching, with thanks said for the fishermen and myself for helping to ensure that Happy got his funeral. There wasn't a dry eye in the church.

You could tell that Father Hogan really cared: he had been shocked by the violence of Happy's death, calling it 'barbaric', and he demanded justice. Father Hogan said he could see why lads like Happy with their lack of education ended up the way they did.

As we filed out of church everyone was shaking Father Hogan's hand, and – being a psychic, and not usually a best friend of the church – I wasn't sure what to do. I was really taken aback when he walked up to me, gave me a hug and said, 'Thank you, Dennis, thank you for all you've done for Mary, and keep up your good work.' I had expected a Catholic priest would want to keep his distance from a psychic, but not this one; this man welcomed me with open arms.

At the service, I met one of Mary's friends, Theresa, and she asked if I could help her, too. Her son, Matthew, has been missing for nine years and I am doing what I can for her, but I don't see an easy conclusion to her tragic story. Matthew was thirty when he vanished in June 1998. He was last seen leaving a pub in Limerick's Roxboro shopping centre.

I have seen Theresa for a reading and told her where I think her son is:

'I'm sorry, my love. But I feel he was killed and buried under a block of houses.'

Her other son was with her and they confirmed that they

think this is likely to be true. It's really tough for them because it's going to be hard, if not impossible, to prove unless those houses are demolished. It's a very difficult case and I am still working on it.

On a subsequent trip to Limerick, I ran into Father Pat at my hotel. He greeted me warmly, saying:

'Hello, Dennis, how are you my friend? I hear you've got Theresa with you this week. Let's hope you can look after her the way you looked after Mary.'

'I'm doing my best, Father Pat,' I assured him. 'I'm doing all I can.'

As a result of the media attention given to my work in the Irish republic, my face has become increasingly well known and people often recognize me when I'm out and about there. During a recent visit to Limerick I went to the post office to cash a postal order: the post office was only 800 yards from the hotel, yet I was stopped five times along the way by folk wanting my autograph or to take my photograph.

As I waited in the queue at the post office, an old lady in front of me kept turning around and looking at me. She asked if I was in a hurry and I told her, truthfully, that I was. She then touched me and said, 'You're the special one, aren't you? I've got to touch you.' When I asked what she meant by 'special' she said, 'You're the one who found Happy.' 'Well,' I told her. 'I helped, but I'm not special.'

Then she shouted to the entire queue of some fifteen people, 'This is the special one and he's in a hurry; you've got to let him to the front.' And it was like the parting of the Red Sea; I went straight to the front to be served.

When I was in Limerick not long ago I held a week of readings during which I saw seventeen mothers, including Theresa, whose sons had been murdered or had died in tragic accidents. There is much talk about the 'Troubles' in Northern Ireland and, of course, many people have died there as a consequence but, I have to say, I've worked on an awful lot of killings in the South.

As well as the seventeen mothers I saw that week, there was a young man in his early twenties and the first words I said to him when he sat down were, 'I've got your brother here and he's telling me he took your bullet.' Again, I had felt the pain of the wound as if it had happened to me – this boy had been shot in the back of the head. His brother looked at me straight and agreed, 'That's right. He did.' He didn't flinch as he said it, yet his sibling had been killed in his place.

His dead brother's spirit was telling me that the killers would soon be after my client and I had to pass on the message:

'You do know that if you stay here you'll be dead within a year, don't you?'

This, too, he accepted in an entirely matter-of-fact fashion. I was really worried about him and wanted to offer him a way out, a chance to escape his killer's bullet. I wanted to throw him a lifeline and so I tried:

'Why don't you come to England with me? My son will give you a job. He is a steel erector. Work hard and you'll earn good money.'

He looked down and said, 'I can't. I can't leave Limerick.'

Now, he's trying to keep his head down and stay away from the gang culture, but that won't change his fate and he knows it.

People come to me because they want to hear the truth. I don't make things up and it's sad, but true, that unless that lad gets out of the country he *will* be dead within a year.

The Many Lives we Live on Earth

Where does life begin and end? I certainly believe in reincarnation – which means literally 'to be made flesh again'. We are reincarnated until the stage at which we have learned all our lessons in life and we cease being reborn on the earth plane and enter the spirit world for good. Once we have learned to surmount or rectify whatever problems and questions our lives throw up, then we don't come back reincarnated in human form again. But if, for example, you are selfish in one life, you will continue to be reborn until you learn to be generous and consider other people. One of the reasons that from time to time I'm not able to contact someone who has passed over is that they are already back here on the earth plane re-learning their lessons!

I read for a young man who was very much in love. He was exceptionally wise and unselfish and he worried that he may not be right for the woman he loved and what she wanted to do in her life. He didn't want to hold her back and was, therefore, willing to let her go. This man demonstrated unconditional love and how many of us can do that? It proved he had learned lessons from a previous life and his unselfishness was such that I would say this will be his last lifetime on the earth plane: when this life ends he will enter the spirit world and remain there.

When we are reborn it tends to be within the same groups of people and very often into the same families, though not necessarily at the same moment in time. A woman from Cambridge told me about a reincarnation in her family. Her mother's spirit came through during her reading and told me about her grandson (my client's son) who had been killed in a motorbike accident. I relayed this information to my client, then at the end of the reading said, 'That wasn't your son I was speaking to.' She told me she knew, and that had I said I was speaking to her son she'd have called me a liar because she had been holding him that morning: 'One thing I am certain about,' she continued, 'is that my son has been reborn as my granddaughter.'

I know something of my previous lives because when I was 'regressed' I spoke with a female voice. So, I know I was a woman and my eight-year-old granddaughter Sky, you recall, sees me as her 'Granny'.

A person's spirit is ageless, whether they died at the age

of one or 101. Some spiritualists believe that the spirits of young children continue to age but, logically, I don't see how that can be. Imagine one person dies crippled by old age at ninety-eight while a healthy two-year-old is killed suddenly. Is that toddler going to continue to grow up in the spirit world? Will the 98-year-old continue to age and grow more decrepit? Of course they won't.

To understand the concept, you have to disregard the ageing process we've always associated with the physical body: the spirit is energy and, in the spirit world, is ageless. However, when spirits show themselves I need to see their physical characteristics in order to recognize who they were. They can choose to adopt the features of themselves at any point between the latest or earliest points of their lives on the earth plane that would have been physically recognizable i.e., they have the power to appear in any form from foetus until the way they looked when they died. For example, someone vain who died at a ripe old age might show themselves to me at their most attractively youthful. Though they're likely to be reborn on the earth plane sooner rather than later to cure them of this vanity!

In terms of what happens to them, the spirits of people who have committed suicide are no different from others who have passed over in that they can still come back – but, according to White Cloud, when they are reborn they will face a magnified version of the same problems that drove them to suicide in the first instance. Until you've learnt your lesson you'll be reborn endlessly to be faced with the same problems you've not managed to deal with in previous lives. It's a bit like failing an exam at school and having to take it again before you can pass the year.

I sometimes read for people who feel suicidal and my heart goes out to them. One man sat slumped with his head in his hands, barely able to summon the energy to speak. I had never seen anyone so low and I empathized with his wretched torment when he said he didn't want to live. At that moment, White Cloud spoke:

'Let me tell you what happens to people like this, Dennis. They cannot run away from their problems by taking their life. When they are reborn they will be back with the same problem, but it will be ten times as hard as in their current lifetime.'

When I told the man this he said he wasn't serious about killing himself and that I shouldn't worry about him. Maybe he changed his mind after what I told him? I have no way of knowing how true White Cloud's words are because I have never regressed anyone who told me they had committed suicide in a previous life.

People who have killed themselves often come through wanting to say sorry to their loved ones. One such spirit was Celine Baldwin's husband, Matthew, who was profusely apologetic for leaving his wife to cope with a mountain of problems.

I met Celine when I was giving readings at an American airbase in Suffolk as part of their Independence Day celebrations. Celine, then in her mid-thirties, introduced herself saying, 'I don't normally go to psychics but a friend said you were the best she had ever seen.'

Straight away, I picked up that she had twin sons but that one of them, Andrew, was autistic, and I could see the everyday struggles and frustrations he encountered: he lacked the confident communication skills of his eight-year-old twin, Mark.

'You know why you've got Andrew, don't you?' I asked, reaching out to hold her hand.

'No,' replied Celine.

'It's because you are strong and therefore you can cope with him and fight for what he needs.'

She wiped away a tear and nodded. Andrew's problems at school were a source of great worry to her and I was able to tell her that, despite the lack of support he was receiving, I knew it would 'all be fine in the end'. And my prediction soon came true when Andrew moved to a much more supportive school.

Since then I have come to know Celine and Andrew well and have given Celine several readings – one of the most memorable being when Matthew's spirit spoke of his heartache at leaving her to cope with the twins. Celine was in the audience at a show I was giving in a village hall. As the spirit came through I started to mimic it stroking its chin, I told the audience I was getting a very strong smell of aftershave and I described a scar on the spirit's lip – which Celine later confirmed was from when a dog had bitten Matthew as a child. When I asked if anyone knew who I was talking about Celine put up her hand.

Matthew loved his family very much but suffered from depression and had attempted suicide twice before. When his spirit came through, he kept repeating how sorry he was for leaving his wife and children to cope without him and for the financial mess he'd left them with. 'I can't say it enough, I am just so sorry for all the hurt I have caused,' was his message to Celine – who was shaking visibly as she listened. Then I added:

'He wants me to congratulate you and say how proud he is of you, Celine. He is proud that you have passed the college course.'

The audience was silent and the atmosphere was highly charged. Celine was overcome with emotion and tears pricked her eyes. Matthew had died before she enrolled to train as a classroom assistant, she had worked her socks off to pass but presumed her late husband would never know about her achievement. Now, he even wanted to give her flowers to celebrate:

'He wants me to give you a bouquet to congratulate you,' I told Celine. 'He knows how much you love flowers, and he wants you to have a bunch of pink carnations with all his love. He also wants you to give his love to "the boysies"; he says that's what he used to call the twins.'

I have told Andrew's mother that I feel Andrew has had links with water and served on a warship during wartime during a previous lifetime and that I can also see a connection with lifeboats. Celine agrees that her son has a strong affinity with water and has noticed on seaside holidays that Andrew takes an avid interest in the lifeboat museum, wherever they find one. He becomes totally absorbed and is fascinated beyond natural curiosity by relics and stories surrounding lifeboats.

Various events support Andrew's previous incarnations. Around a year after I'd mentioned the link with water and the warship his art therapy teacher was compelled to discuss with Celine a picture Andrew had drawn. Using a blue pen to make large, swirling circles he first drew a choppy sea, then he picked up a red pen and became angry and agitated, whacking the pen down onto the paper, and making noises like explosions and shouting, 'This is the blood of all the people on the boat being killed by bombs.'

When he spent the day on a friend's canal boat, though he had never been on one before, he knew exactly how to operate the lock. When the family were on holiday in Devon, he started singing an old sea shanty that Celine was sure he had never heard before, and when he watches any film with a ship in it, he can describe technical details about the ship and its engines using nautical engineering terminology.

Regressing someone can produce fascinating information concerning their previous lives. People are often curious to know about this aspect of their past and I can send them on this voyage deep into the unknown. To regress a client I first hypnotize them into a deep, trance-like state; this opens up their subconscious. I then gently ask them who they are and they will reply as the person they have been: they will take on the voice and whatever language they used in their previous life.

In Newmarket I regressed a young woman who spoke about owning a furniture shop in Bury St Edmunds and described her children and her life more than a hundred years ago. She gave the name of the street the shop was in and, later, I did some research and discovered that the shop had, indeed, existed in the 19th century. It meant she had also acquired some new relatives to research.

Onstage at Harrow Arts Centre I regressed a woman who had been a teenager during the Great Plague in England in 1665. She told us her name and gave a vivid description of the painful deaths she witnessed – the terrible sickness and the fear of the Black Death that prevailed – and she repeatedly said she was starving and had little to eat. She brought history to life for everyone there and it was really very moving.

Some women from Romford came to me for regression. One turned out to have been a Danish woodcutter. She spoke in a deep, husky voice and in Danish – which I couldn't understand a word of – but she was clear that's what she had been, she remembered everything about it and she thought it was hilarious.

It was, however, one of the other women's regression that was truly amazing. When I regressed her I could see she was in a deep trance but I couldn't get her to talk about a previous life anywhere which was really most unusual. Again, I asked, 'Who are you? Can you tell me where you are, love?' Her reply was incredible and left me speechless: 'I'm in the spirit world.'

I thought, 'This is it, this is where I get a real look into the spirit world.' This had never happened to me before. I don't know of any psychic who has any idea what the spirit world is really like: none of us is able to venture into that sphere. Spirits come to us from that world but they don't tell us anything about it.

But the woman's soft voice changed and out came this hard, clipped German accent and I recognized it instantly:

'This regression ends here, Dennis, right now. You are looking where you shouldn't be looking.'

'Is that you, Jagna?'

'Yes, it's me, Dennis.'

I could not believe this had happened. Jagna had, somehow, come through this woman and was telling me the regression must end; I was not permitted to look into the spirit world. I had no choice but to do as she said.

When the woman came round I asked if she remembered anything that had happened and she said, 'The only thing I can remember is that I kept getting the name Jagna and wanting to be in Germany', which confirmed that my guide had come through this woman to tell me to stop.

Even though I have no specific knowledge of what it's like in the spirit world, I'm of the opinion that it is a lovely place. The only thing I wonder is, that if it's as good as I think it is, then none of us would be here on the earth plane. Why would we sit here in this world of shit and pain and cruelty when we could be there? We wouldn't, and I think that is the reason we don't have any memory of the spirit world.

Woman's Own:
Ghostbuster In-Residence

For two years, 2005–6, I was the resident 'super psychic' for the UK publication *Woman's Own*, where readers would write in asking me to investigate strange happenings, contact their loved ones or to give guidance. The letters would be sent to the magazine where they picked the most interesting. They would then supply me with the most basic information possible – enough to get me to the right place and no more. Like I've said before, I don't like to be given extra details beforehand, preferring to remain 'cocooned' so that I can use my psychic abilities in a completely pure and unprejudiced way.

Everyone has their ups and downs, that's life, but Trisha Goddard, queen of the confessional on Channel Five TV, has had more than her fair share of heartache – including a string of violent relationships, a nervous breakdown that put her in a psychiatric unit for two years, her youngest sister's suicide and more. Goddard makes no secret of the hardship she has suffered; she talks about it openly on her daytime TV show and has written a no-holds-barred auto-biography.

In my role for *Woman's Own*, the magazine asked me to do a reading for Goddard in January 2006 to tie in with a new Channel Five series *Britain's Psychic Challenge*. Trisha was presenting the show, which aimed to test the psychics' skills, and the first programme would air that month. She had last had a psychic reading at the age of seventeen and it had turned out to be a load of rubbish. Thirty-one years later I hoped I wouldn't disappoint her.

Breathless and apologetic, Trisha arrived half an hour late for our appointment at a hotel in Norwich, but as soon as she walked into the room I was bowled over by her bright smile.

Being late had obviously upset her busy schedule, 'I've got twenty minutes and that's it, so we need to do this and be done,' she said, then asked her PA to fetch her when the time was up. A reading would normally last for thirty to sixty minutes, so twenty was really pushing it but, 'Okay, love, let's get started,' I said.

When we met I knew very little about Trisha's past, but during the reading I was able to impart lots of personal information about her parents, her daughters, her ex-husband and her sister, alongside observations about how she had fought so many demons and faced such horrendous challenges in life.

When her PA opened the door to say, 'Time's up,' Trisha told her, 'No, I'm not ready,' and asked her to go and feed the parking meter. Enthralled by the detail I was telling of her past and present life, she wanted to hear more. Another twenty minutes flew by and there was another knock on the door and, yet again, Trisha called:

'I'm not ready. Go and put more money in the meter.'

I reassured Trisha about certain issues she was dealing with and told her about a very hush-hush deal which was on the table. I'd read for her for almost two hours – one of the longest readings I have ever done – and the experience had been hugely emotional for her. She had found the information I'd given about her children particularly helpful and, clearly far from disappointed, she thanked me profusely saying, 'You hit it right on the head.'

In the follow-on interview published five weeks later in *Woman's Own* she spoke very positively:

'It's not easy for psychics to convince me as my life is an open book. It's always going to be hard for them to impress me because I would constantly be wondering if they'd just done a lot of research. But I am impressed with Dennis.'

'Perhaps the thing that amazed me the most was that

Dennis was able to be quite specific about a job offer I've received. He also got my personality and those of my children spot on.'

'*I don't suffer fools gladly, but if I'm bored, you'd never guess. Dennis told me that only three or four people know me well enough to know when I'm faking interest. He's right! I might look the life and soul of the party, but in reality there's going to be hell to pay. I suppose it's my inner bitch.'*

Reading for Trisha had been a very great pleasure and I feel she has a strong spiritual side to her, so I was delighted when I read her kind words.

I've been to some strange haunted houses in my time but one that stands out in my mind was Rachel and Martin Skinner's home on a council estate in Wakefield. The couple lived with their children, Jess, two, and Lucy, three, in a house which looked not unlike my own – to all intents and purposes an ordinary pebbledash building – but while mine is home to one spirit, this one had four – and they were each so very different.

I visited in February 2006 after Rachel and Martin had contacted me at *Woman's Own* because they were experiencing so many spooky goings-on in their house. They wanted me to investigate and hoped I could put a stop to their supernatural disruption: things had been going missing and would reappear a few hours later; they'd heard foot-steps on the stairs and the children's stair gate opening and closing; mirrors had been flying off the walls; clocks went haywire and light bulbs blew. They also described a small ghost in the house.

I knew nothing about this in advance of my visit (as usual with my work for *Woman's Own* all I'd been given were directions to the house) but as I walked around I soon picked up the spirit of a little girl:

'I feel strongly that she is linked to Jess, and her hair is dark blond like his,' I told the couple.

'Actually, I think she's his twin. I'm sure this little girl is around all the time and all of you will have seen her. There's nothing to worry about, though, she isn't evil, just a bit mischievous. But I imagine things go missing and later reappear, and I expect you hear her moving around upstairs.'

Martin and Rachel were flabbergasted: I had described exactly some of the spooky happenings they had noticed. Then Rachel told me that when she was first pregnant with Jess she had had some bleeding and had 'always wondered whether I might have lost his twin'. In my experience, the spirit of a foetus can make its presence felt, and that's what had happened here. Lucy, I discovered, had been talking about a girl who she said was called Ben and whispered to her when she was asleep and wanted to play with her; Ben could well be Lucy's little sister.

I then picked up the spirit of a man in his sixties called Sandy living in the living room on the ground floor. I told the Skinners that there was a musty smell and a drop in temperature which came and went depending upon when he was around, and that I felt he was linked to Martin. The connection felt so strong that I believe it may have been his twin. Upstairs in the couple's bedroom I felt the presence of a second spirit which I was certain belonged to Rachel's grandmother:

'I know you two didn't get on, so I don't know why she is around. I think she hasn't realized it's time to move on,' I told Rachel.

'Also, the sweet wrappers you've found are hers,' I said, and Rachel confirmed that, yes, her grandmother did have a sweet tooth.

There was more startling news to come. In another of the bedrooms I saw a young man hanging from a loft hatch above the bed and he said, 'It's about time you've come. I'm sick of hanging around here.' I kid you not, those were his exact words to me. There was no hatch visible in the bedroom ceiling, but when I told the Skinners what I'd seen they explained that the previous owner had covered it over and that, once, a boy had hung himself from it. In happier days, apparently, the boy had been a bit of a joker, which explained his quip about his suicide.

Martin and Rachel wanted me to clear the house of spirits, apart from the little girl:

'We've become quite attached to her,' said Rachel. 'We'd miss her if she went. But we do want to get rid of smelly Sandy, my Gran and the lad who killed himself.'

I was glad they wanted to keep the little girl with them. I then called on Jagna and White Cloud to help clear the house – they would do their work through me. I closed my eyes and focused hard on the job in hand and felt my guides' energies passing through my body.

Freed of the unwanted spirits the Skinner family should now have the peace they craved. The smell would go now that Sandy's spirit had gone and, as the young lad had told me, he wanted to leave the house so I know we did him a favour. But I have to admit that when I went to get rid of Gran's spirit I couldn't find her. I have to hope she decided to go of her own will and that she won't be back.

Rachel thanked me saying, 'I can't wait to tell the neighbours about the ghosts. It gives the house something special.

'I'm just glad I'm not going crazy. I've never really been scared, but now I can stop worrying. I just hope Gran knows she's not wanted in my bedroom.'

There is a first time for everything and a letter to *Woman's Own* from Claire Powell prompted my first visit to a haunted shed. However, it was no joking matter: this particular spirit was making life miserable for schoolboy Peter Powell and in desperation his mother asked me to visit their home in Hornchurch.

It wasn't even an old shed and from the moment his mother bought it for Peter to use as a workshop, strange things had started to happen without and within. They had heard the sound of gravel being thrown at the window and seen a black tar-like substance mysteriously ooze down the glass and then vanish without trace. Claire worried that she couldn't make sense of it and, at first, kept thinking there must be a rational explanation.

But that wasn't all. An inexplicable black haze had gathered at the startled boy's feet and crept up toward his waist – which naturally terrified him – plus tools jumped off their hooks onto the floor and objects would topple off the shelves.

As if that wasn't enough, Claire had seen a black silhouette moving around the house and her son's bed shaking violently. No wonder it was getting too much for her. Then, the final straw for mother and son was Peter being kicked in the back by 'someone' in the shed – and he had a bruise to prove it.

As was the form, prior to my visit I knew no more than the fact that 'spooky things' had been freaking out Claire and Peter and they wanted me to restore normality. I sensed when we met that both Claire and Peter possessed strong psychic ability – they were clairsentient, which enabled them to feel the presence of a spirit, and that was why they'd been subject to such a degree of aggravation.

Claire was very relieved when I realized that no evil spirit was to blame for all the mayhem. The culprit, I told her, was, 'Standing right behind me and his name is Jack.' I continued:

'He's from the Victorian era. There was a house here then, but where Peter's shed stands now, there was a tree that Jack liked to sit under. He's furious that someone is invading what he considers his space. He's not evil, he's just a very grumpy old man.'

'So, we crowded him out then, did we? No wonder he was so angry with Peter,' said an albeit astonished Claire.

I sensed straight away that Jack was with me and following my every move as I walked around the Powells' house, but it was time for him to move on and leave this family alone.

'He knows why I'm here and he's not happy,' I said. 'I'm not going to ask him politely to leave, my spirit guides are going to make him go to the light and leave you alone.'

I called on Jagna and White Cloud to pass their energy through me and after five minutes felt that Jack had gone. I told Claire she needn't worry about him any longer. I assumed that the disruption had undoubtedly affected Peter's school work and Claire concurred.

'Just as well we got rid of him when we did,' I told her. 'He would have fed more and more off Peter's energy and grown increasingly violent – Peter wouldn't have been able to get a wink of sleep, either.'

Absolute proof of Jack's departure came when Peter, home from school, walked through the front door and said:

'It's gone, Mum. What's happened?'

Christmas was coming and while most people look forward to the joy of the festive season it can be a poignant time for those missing loved ones; a time to reminisce and remember. June Halford was feeling sad when she wrote to *Woman's Own*.

Driving to Ely to read for her, I noticed an unexpected passenger sitting on the back seat – a black guy in his twenties, with a beard. This, as you know, sometimes happens and the passenger will have a connection with the person I am going to read for. Each time I glanced in my rearview mirror, the guy winked at me.

When I arrived at June's house and she opened the door, I was surprised to see that she was white; I'd sensed a strong connection with the black guy. When I told June that her son was coming through to me, and that he was black, she explained that his father was black, too – and the penny dropped, it just hadn't occurred to me.

It was a very emotional reading for June because her son,

Marcus, had passed away on Christmas Day 2004 almost a year before the day on which we met. This Christmas, the first without him, was proving hard for her but she was surrounded by family and when I told them all about Marcus hitching a ride they laughed and said he was always winking, 'as if to let everyone in on a wonderful joke'.

Marcus had died suddenly at the home he shared with his girlfriend and her son, Nicholas. An otherwise healthy twenty-seven year-old, he suffered from some type of seizure and one of these fits had caused his heart to stop. As June showed me photographs of her handsome son, his spirit came through to me. As always when working for the magazine, I was working with a blank canvas.

June was immensely reassured when Marcus passed on the message that he 'never felt a thing' when his heart stopped. I put the time of death at a quarter past five in the evening. A later time is given on the death certificate because following Marcus's heart attack attempts were made to resuscitate him but 'he was dead long before that,' June told me. He had also, I told June, already made contact with his girlfriend, speaking through the voice of her son Nicholas.

I finished the reading by passing on a message from Marcus who wanted to say, 'Goodbye, Mam, from your ever loving son,' In the last Christmas card he had sent his mother he had written, 'Happy Christmas, from your ever loving son'.

My reading was not, however, the first time Marcus's mother had heard from her son since he died. On the day before his funeral June had answered the phone and, 'Hello, Mam,' said the voice at the other end. It was Marcus without a doubt – he had lived in Birmingham for a while and picked up a distinctive twang – 'I'm all right, don't you worry,' he'd told his mother. She handed over the phone to her youngest son Jermaine and he, too, heard Marcus's voice — and then the voice changed and it was Nicholas calling to talk about funeral arrangements.

'Yes, that was Marcus,' I said. 'He wanted you to know he is still around.'

With tears in her eyes June admitted she'd told few people about Marcus's call because she knew they'd think she was 'going mad with grief'. 'But,' she told the assembled company, 'I know what I heard, and Dennis has confirmed it.'

June wanted to spend the first anniversary of her son's death at the crematorium. She said:

'On Boxing Day last year we threw away all the decorations. I'm not planning on celebrating Christmas this year.'

I was adamant that Marcus would not want that:

'He wants the family to celebrate, and at quarter past five on Christmas Day you should all raise your glasses to him.'

Then I gave June a hug goodbye and a reminder to, 'have a merry Christmas for Marcus'.

It's great when I can relate to their loved ones the funny stories spirits tell of when they were alive. Being able to pass these on was one the most enjoyable things about my time working with *Woman's Own*.

There was a boy in spirit aged about thirteen, for example, who told with glee that when he was playing football with his grandmother in her garden, she went to kick the ball, missed it, then fell over and broke her back.

'No, I actually fell over and broke my coccyx, not my back,' his grandmother later told me. 'And I was in sheer agony.'

'Well, he's still laughing about it. I can see him as plain as day thinking how hilarious it was.'

Then she, too, laughed, remembering how the boy had been in fits of laughter, 'and there was me rolling around the ground in agony'.

The magazine sent me off on a ghost hunt at a hotel and, even before I set foot in it, I knew the spirits didn't want me there. As I was about to swing into the car park at the George and Dragon in West Wycombe, Buckinghamshire, I lost control over the steering wheel. It was as if someone else had taken over and was driving, deliberately, into the wall. Crash. My PA, travelling in her own car to meet me, also had an accident – her first ever – and her car barely limped the last lap to the hotel.

The hotel, a traditional 18th-century coaching inn with wooden beams and open fires, had provided shelter to generations of weary travellers, traders and tourists and I sensed many secrets within its heart – some of them shamelessly immoral.

A mass of energies stirred as soon as I stepped over the threshold and I sensed not just one spirit but four or five, including a particularly nasty one. A shiver slid down my spine and an overwhelming sadness surrounded me.

In the bar I pointed to an empty table by the window; just looking at it made me shudder:

'I would bet that anybody who sits there for any length of time ends up feeling depressed,' I said, and the barman agreed, telling me customers complained of feeling 'uncomfortable' at the table and few regulars ever sat there.

It seemed to me that the inn had been frequented by members of the Hellfire Club, a notorious assembly of 18th-century aristocrats with a reputation for debauchery. They'd meet at the inn before heading for some nearby caves where they would perform pseudo-satanic religious ceremonies and have orgies. They had left their vile spirits behind and I was feeling their energies strongly in the bar area:

'They might be high-born, but I'm afraid they are cruel,'

I said. 'They can buy their way out of anything and don't have much regard for anyone they deem socially inferior.'

When I also sensed the spirit of influential American statesman Benjamin Franklin and asked what he might have to do with the place, it turned out he had an eye for the ladies and was a member of the Hellfire Club, too. I was shocked.

Now, I know some of the things I talk about sound far fetched, but I don't invent what I see and hear from the spirit world and that includes Sukie the barmaid whose saucy spirit popped up next – complete with ample bosoms which she flaunted to tease the local lads and customers.

'Her name is Suzie, or Sukie – that's the name coming through,' I said. 'I see her behind the bar, flirting and catching pennies in her cleavage. She is incredibly mischievous.'

I then walked up a very ornate staircase, stopping off on each landing to look around the rooms. Just before I reached the top flight, I felt a spirit trying to push me back with such force that it stopped me in my tracks. I wondered, would Judith feel the same force? Without telling her why, I led her up the stairs and at exactly the same spot as it stopped me, a mysterious force blocked her progress:

'Oh my God,' she gasped. 'What was that?'

'Someone clearly doesn't want me to reach that top floor, that's what,' I told her.

But using all my energy I managed, step by determined

step, to reach the top step. There, I came upon the spirit of a man wearing high-cut leather boots and who told me his name was Sam. Identifying and interpreting smells is a very important part of clairsentience because it adds so much about the person's life. On Sam I smelled hay and hops and, feeling he worked with horses and stables, deduced he was the head groom – and that he certainly liked a beer.

My vision of Sam vanished and I entered another room which contained the spirit of a mischievous boy called Enoch: he was a real monkey, always up to tricks. The pictures which flashed before my mind's eye showed a boy about nine years old in the hayloft where he slept. I was telling Judith this would be a room to avoid because Enoch would want to play and would try to get your attention. 'This boy would play tricks all night, he would be moving things around and — '

A sudden, searing pressure rolled across my chest and I believed I knew how the boy died and said:

'I feel he had a violent death, that he was run over by the wheels of a cart. The wheels crushed him and that is how the poor lad died.'

Unbeknown to me, the hotel was holding a ghost-busting event in Enoch's room that evening. I was invited to join in, but said I'd rather sit at the back of the room and observe – I'd said nothing about what I knew of Enoch and his hayloft.

At midnight, four people sat around the table. They placed a wine glass at its centre, encircled by letters of the alphabet which would, they hoped, allow any spirit they might contact to spell answers to their questions. Each person placed a finger on the base of the glass and asked if any spirits were present. I watched in amazement as the glass glided across the table until letter by letter was spelled, ENOCH: he certainly didn't want to be ignored.

Through answers to various questions Enoch's spirit said he loved to play and that he had met a violent death at the hands of a stranger. The guests then asked him to move the glass toward the person booked to sleep in his room that night whereupon he selected the correct occupant.

At one o'clock in the morning I was ready to leave when the barman asked me a favour:

'Would you come and look at my room in the staff quarters, Dennis? My partner and I get the most awful feelings in that room and we have terrible rows in it. I hate sleeping there, there's something really nasty about it.'

I followed him:

'You're not kidding it's nasty,' I told him. 'I guarantee you'll feel a lot better if I get rid of this thing. I can see it at the end of the bed, watching me. It's an evil spirit and it is not human.'

I agreed to do my best to get rid of this foul spirit – to 'clear' the room – but I knew it would not be a pleasant job. Every time I have worked on clearing evil spirits such as this one I've ended up bruised and cut all over – anyone who says spirits can't hurt you is wrong.

I went outside the building and did what I could, calling on Jagna and White Cloud to remove the evil presence once and for all, so that this bloke and his partner could find some peace. I felt my guides push through me their energy that would flush out the evil; their energy drove on until a stillness fell and the atmosphere became one of peace.

My mission of mercy accomplished, I couldn't wait to get some sleep, but there was no way I'd get so much as a wink in that place – far too many lively spirits who would all want a chat. So, I jumped into my car with the smashed front and said goodbye to the ghostly gaggle who watched me drive off before returning to haunt and bewilder the hotel guests.

The Body in the River

A new client, a blonde, middle-aged woman named Sally Perrin sat before me. She had driven for three hours from her home in Shropshire for a reading with me here, in Cambridgeshire, in January 2006. To discover why she sought a reading, I settled into my favoured position – on my tummy on the sofa – and prepared to connect with the spirit world. I didn't mince my words:

'You've had a shit year, my dear, absolutely shit. You couldn't have had a worse one. I'm going to really upset you – the next one isn't much better.'

Sally looked at me and nodded agreement. Within seconds I could see why this woman was suffering so much trauma and my heart went out to her as the reasons why her life had crumbled came through to me: over the past eighteen months she had been to hell and back, time and time again.

I could see that she had lost her son and that he wasn't in this country. My clairsentience was helping me see, hear and feel what had happened to him. The reading continued:

'What was the violence with your son's death? Was he away when it happened? I see him being away. I am feeling that he was killed and that it was over something silly, something really silly.'

Tears welled up in Sally's eyes and she replied:

'I just don't know, what happened to Blake is still a mystery.'

Blake's spirit came through – blond hair, broad grin and he was wearing steel-framed glasses – bringing more detail to the reading:

'He's been missing for a while now, hasn't he? This didn't happen yesterday, it's coming up for two years ago. He keeps showing me poplar trees; I've got a road that runs straight through the poplar trees and I've got grass to the left. It's a little road, more like a rough track. And there's a pond, or still water, there, too: there's a pond on the left and he's near the pond. I can also see a building on the left. Is there a "Saint" in the name of the place?'

Then, through Blake's spirit and clairsentience, I felt cold water, and gasping for air, and sinking and drowning deep under a torrent of murky water. My stomach churned to say it, but I had to tell Blake's mother everything that was coming through to me:

'I'm so sorry, my love, but I've got to tell you he is dead. He is showing me a river, a deep and fast-flowing river.'

Sally would never see her son again, and now she knew it without doubt: the reading she had sought confirmed the dread in her heart.

'He's sending you his love, Sally,' I told her.

Blake was Sally's son by her first marriage. Two days after his twenty-fifth birthday Blake Hartley, an officer cadet at Sandhurst, had mysteriously disappeared in the early hours of 8 August 2004. He was expedition leader on an army training exercise in Chamonix in the French Alps and vanished only hours after the team of nine cadets had arrived and set up camp.

For Sally there was a wealth of unanswered questions about her son's disappearance. The best thing to do, I knew, was to go with Sally to Chamonix and help find her son's body. Reading for his mother within the area Blake had disappeared would certainly bring forth more information.

I was as ignorant of Chamonix as I had been of Wichita, but soon realized how suited the area would be to a man of action and lover of extreme sports such as Blake. The small town in the foothills of Mont Blanc is the heart of the famous ski resort, while the huge valley and mountain ranges of the area straddle the borders of France, Switzerland

and Italy. Everything about the terrain here is on a grand scale and as well as organized sport for tourists – snowboarding, white water rafting, climbing – there are vast tracts of empty, remote country.

Four months after meeting Sally, Judith and I flew to Geneva. I no longer feared flying, but I didn't feel good – asthma and backache – when we arrived around midnight and in pouring rain. We drove for a couple of hours and arrived at the hotel in Chamonix around half past two in the morning. Everyone had gone to bed, of course, so we had to hike our luggage up to our rooms on the fourth floor. It nearly killed me; every step jarred through my aching back.

I was really feeling the after-effects of the car accident I'd had all those years ago and that, along with being a fat bastard, the narrow winding stairs and the absence of a lift, proved the bane of my stay at that hotel: I had to psych myself up every time I had to climb those stairs. It was a mental and physical challenge and I'd have to stop at least ten times before I got to my room. I would stand at the bottom, doubled up with back pain, looking up and thinking, 'It's impossible. I just can't do it.' We were only there for the weekend, but it was quite long enough for my aching back.

For what little remained of my first night in Chamonix I slept really badly and my first thought on waking was of breakfast: an English breakfast, the full works. Unseasoned traveller that I am, I thought that as France is famed for its food, that surely wouldn't be a problem. I was deeply disappointed when I discovered that the French don't do 'English' breakfast. When, eventually, I found a café where they said they'd fry up some eggs and bacon, I'd never seen anything like it: the egg was uncooked and then there was this little piece of pork. I went somewhere else and had coffee, a coke and a croissant which cost twenty-six euros; extortionate.

Chamonix did not impress me that weekend in May: I didn't enjoy my French breakfasts; my back was agony throughout; the hotel stairs were torture and the rain poured down for the duration of our visit.

Judith and I met up with Sally in the town centre. Her second husband, David, plus two of his kids, Alex and Nina – both adults – were with her, along with a reporter and a cameraman from ITV Central news who she had organized to record events. In the summer of 2003, the year before he died, Blake had spent three months based in Chamonix as part of a mountaineering expedition. He had thoroughly enjoyed his stay in the lively resort full of stylish clubs, restaurants and bars and, with his love of sport – climbing and white water rafting in particular – he had made the most of the mountain ranges and the spate rivers.

When he returned to Chamonix in August 2004, Blake

was in charge of the team of eight fellow cadets. Having made camp at a local site, on the evening he died, the cadets went into town for a night out. I had asked Sally to start me off somewhere that Blake would have been that night, and I would pick it up from there and feel my way along as if in his footsteps. I don't know how I do it, but when I put in my mind the intention to follow a route taken by someone, my mind goes there and, thus, I'm able to visualize it as it was at that time. It's almost as if my clairsentience allows me to become the person and to see, hear and feel whatever they experienced.

Sally took me to a spot on a street where Blake and his companions were known to have been and Blake came through to me. Seeing him look proud, I felt he'd had some good news from Sandhurst, and when I asked Sally what this might be, she told me he had recently been awarded his full colours: he had won them for outstanding achievement in climbing when he represented Sandhurst in a national competition. She added that he had, of course, also been delighted to have wangled this trip to Chamonix and so, as far as he was concerned, life 'couldn't have been better'.

As I continued in Blake's footsteps, the name Chris Bonington kept coming through – Sally explained that her son had read every book the famous mountaineer had ever written.

We walked on, in the rain, until I felt compelled to turn suddenly left off the main street, and some 200 yards on I stopped outside a nightclub's red door – on a wall beside it was a poster showing Blake's face and appealing for information. I saw that there had been trouble here; I could hear people arguing. I told Sally what I was getting:

'It's hot in the club and Blake wants to take his drink, a bottle or a glass, outside. The bouncer has told him "no" and Blake is giving him a bit of banter.

'But one of Blake's mates is being gobby and causing friction. Blake's still talking to the bouncer and his mate is trying out his French, welcoming everybody into the club. The bouncer doesn't like it, they're all arguing and Blake's mate is giving it a bit too much lip.'

Sally confirmed my findings and we continued to the end of the road where I turned left, walked a short distance and stopped. Here, I explained to Sally, was where Blake stopped for a pee and then turned around and went back, with the other cadets, to the main street he (and we) had started from. We, now, did the same and stopped at a pizzeria.

I felt Blake and two others wanted to eat there but it was closed – no surprise as it was about two in the morning. They'd had quite a bit to drink and they were all – though mainly the gobby bloke – banging on the restaurant windows. Then Blake began trying to steer them away; he was telling them to leave it. I felt he realized it was getting too loutish

The next lap of our journey brought us to an alley which led directly to the campsite. Here, rather than walk straight up the alley when they returned to camp, I felt the men had walked alongside the river – so, that's the road we now took. I think then, they cut back onto the alley.

At the campsite I stopped briefly where the tents had been pitched. I felt very strongly that Blake had headed back toward the river and so I, too, made for it, walking fast, as Blake would have been – as if trying to keep up with him as I follow his final steps. I turn into a little lane, then march through someone's garden. I say to Sally:

'I've got Blake coming through here. But this garden's changed. In my mind I've got it overgrown.'

'Bang on,' confirms Sally and tells me what is now a garden was wasteland in the summer of 2004.

I feel we are very close, just seconds away from discovering how Blake Hartley died. I stride from the garden, across the road and come to a halt by the fast-flowing river – exactly as I had pictured it. I tell Sally and the others:

'Here, right here. This is where it happened.'

I focused hard on the clairsentient thoughts whirring through my mind like a slide show. I feel he met someone. I feel a push, then a punch gets thrown then there's a sharp crack. At the reading for Sally in Cambridgeshire, when the pictures of Blake's death flashed through my mind I thought it was murder, now I doubted it.

There is great tension as Sally asks, 'What happened? Was he knocked in the river?'

I am still asking myself: Did he fall, or was he pushed? Then Jagna and Blake both come through with more information and my body grows fiercely cold as I sink under the weight of the torrent. I walk away from the river's edge and a sharp pain stabs at the back of my head. My gaze fixes on a huge boulder and I'm rubbing the back of my head and saying, 'I want to hit my head on that rock.'

I tell Sally that during a fist fight, her son hit his head on that rock then, already unconscious, he fell into the river and drowned. I tell her that I believe her son's death was not murder but a terrible and tragic accident.

Blake Hartley's death had been investigated by the army, and by French police: foul play was ruled out. When the ITV reporter interviewed her about what she'd thought of my investigation and verdict Sally made it clear that she was impressed by what I'd told her and was effusive in her praise: 'Dennis has just astounded us'; 'He has come up with everything'. And his mother pointed up the fact that Blake had been white water rafting in Chamonix the summer before her died and knew the safety drill regarding capsize: 'If he had not hit his head,' she said. 'He would have stood a chance.'

* * *

My next challenge that weekend in May was to find Blake's body. This was Sally's fourth visit to Chamonix trying to piece together the events surrounding her son's death and in the hope his body would be found. Blake's body had been so long in the water, we could expect to find only its remains and Sally understood this grim reality, but I wanted to help her find whatever I could because that helps to bring all-important closure for those left behind.

That morning, while we had been retracing Blake's steps, a group of Blake's friends had flown in; they'd just dropped everything and jumped on a plane to be there for him – one of them had forgotten his wallet and another arrived wearing a Hawaiian shirt and flip flops with no spare clothes. They were friends from university plus a couple from the Oxford Officer Training Corps and two of his cousins. The fact so many had turned up because, they said, they knew that Blake would do the same for them, said a lot about the kind of person he was.

I had my own picture of Blake in my mind, but I wanted Sally to tell me about her son:

'Blake was happy, always happy,' she said. 'I never saw him angry. He was always helpful and a lovely person to have around.

'David is not much use on the old DIY, but Blake was very practical and could turn his hand to anything. I would save up little jobs for him, and he would always do them so willingly and competently.'

Sally told me Blake had read Rural Resource Management at Reading University then had taken a gap-year and taught outdoor activities at Timbertops school in Australia. He had changed his plans of a future in agriculture and went, instead, to Canada on a glacier-climbing expedition and did some cross-country skiing.

She explained that Blake had joined the Royal Military Academy at Sandhurst six months before the Chamonix trip. He had completed his second term there, at the end of which cadets are required to organize an expedition and, because he had passed his mountain leadership courses in Wales he'd been selected as team leader on the Chamonix expedition. Blake had thought it a great idea to get the army to pay for him to go on, effectively, a climbing holiday:

'He was absolutely chuffed to be going back to Chamonix,' said Sally. 'He was as happy as Larry and so looking forward to it. He even planned to stay on after the expedition and do some serious climbing on his own.'

After the morning piecing together the events surrounding Blake's death, in the afternoon we embarked on the search for his body. Clairsentience had helped pinpoint a likely location. I was looking for the place I had first described to Sally in Cambridgeshire: with a stretch of still water with pebbles and a little island in the middle, beside a poplar-tree-lined road and close to a village with 'Saint' in its name – luckily, the Chamonix area contains few villages so named. I felt strongly that Blake's body was in still water, but that the river he had drowned in had been in spate and carried his body into a lake.

We drank coffee at a roadside café and spread out the map on the table, though I had no idea how to pronounce the place names. I felt a mix of trepidation and excitement – I wanted to be right and I was confident about the site I'd envisaged.

Sally suggested we aim south of Bonneville because a body had twice been sighted there. Sally had told me that the police had seen a body not too far from Bonneville after Blake drowned. And ten days after the drowning a man named Joseph Dancet had also reported a body floating under a bridge in Bonneville. Joseph's sighting prompted a ground and helicopter search, and police did see the body underwater, not far from the lane I'd described – but with the river in full spate, it proved impossible to reach and the search was abandoned.

This upset Joseph but it was a devastating blow for Sally and her family who, already, felt helpless and isolated as they tried to deal with officialdom in a language, system and country all foreign to them. As it turns out from the descriptions given by both Joseph and the police, the different sight-

Dennis McKenzie

ings were of the same corpse. I found Bonneville on the map hoping to see a 'Saint' somewhere close by, and there was a village called Scientrier where I felt we should look. In the French Alps and close to Geneva, Scientrier was less than an hour's drive from Chamonix. The River Arve runs a narrow course through Chamonix then widens as it reaches the Bonneville basin and I felt Blake's body had been carried north into that area. But there, because the river was thick with silt, the body might not have been spotted.

We drove north, stopping at various different streams and rivers, but none of them felt right. Then we pulled in to a lay-by so Nina, who was pregnant, and others could use the toilet. We were by the edge of a lake and facing a sheer cliff face. As I waited in the car with David's son, Alex, Blake's spirit came through – he was climbing fearlessly up the most precarious face of the cliff. I knew Blake was an accomplished climber, but I felt this particular cliff must be significant. I relayed all this to Alex, but he said nothing until Sally and David returned then asked me to tell them what I'd said. Sally's response explained the significance: 'That was his favourite place in the world. That was his practice climb. He used to climb it regularly during the time he'd spent in Chamonix.' My observation sent a tingle up Alex's spine – and mine, too. I looked again at the cliff and wondered at Blake's ability, though to me it seemed more like lunacy.

We continued driving around and around. I knew we weren't far from the location I had pictured, but it was starting to get dark and everyone was tired and pretty drained. Nevertheless, keen for a result, I wanted to keep looking so we carried on – and, in a brief respite from the rain, the countryside looked glorious as the sun lit up mountain and river valley. Suddenly, I felt we were within moments of reaching our destination:

'Down there,' I told David who was driving. 'Turn right down that track.'

There it was, the little poplar-tree-lined track. David stopped the car and I leaped out, marched down the track and, guided by clairsentience, hurried on until some thick bushes at the foot of the track barred my way. The others had caught up with me by the time I was pushing aside the branches to reveal – a river. It was identical to the scene I had pictured in my mind; I could see the pebbles and the little island in the middle. And the still water. The river had flooded the island in the spring snowmelt leaving pools in the hollows.

The site was very close to where Sally and the police had already painstakingly searched, but she was not sure if they had covered this specific area. Yet again, I felt the familiar drowning sensation and knew this place had a connection with Blake.

I was convinced part of Blake's body was on that island in the river:

'This whole area needs searching,' I said. 'And five hundred metres on either side in the river. I don't feel it has been searched properly.'

The TV reporter asked for Sally's thoughts at this stage and she seemed pleased enough, saying she felt 'relieved and hopeful' because it was not a large area to search. 'We were up here before with twelve or fifteen men,' she went on. 'But I don't know where they searched.'

The next day we met with the local police chief to ask if he would organize another search and I explained why I felt this location was so important. He was very open minded and agreed to dive once more on the site we'd identified. The police officer spoke only French, so his English girl-friend translated for us. I said, 'It must be very, very strange working with a psychic.' 'Not as strange as working with criminals,' he replied. He had a very dry sense of humour.

Four months later, when the water levels had dropped sufficiently, the police searched the spot I'd identified. Nothing was found on the island. However two femurs were discovered in the river where I'd told the police diver to search. I still believe that if further searches are carried out then more of his body will be discovered.

Before we left Chamonix, I suggested we hold a séance, which is something I do very rarely because the spirits come through to me anyway. This, however, would be a séance with a difference: instead of Blake's spirit coming through me, I wanted to see if he would come to us through Alex, his stepbrother. Alex is five years older than Blake and was very close to him – and Alex has some psychic ability.

I always know when someone has the ability because I feel it radiate from them. In fact, I disappoint a lot of people I read for who have thought themselves psychic when I tell them they are not; but I surprise others who have not realized they are psychic until I tell them they are.

Alex readily agreed to take part in the transmediumship. Transmediumship is when a person goes into a trance and the spirit speaks through their mouth and, though it is not something I specialize in, I wanted to try in order to give Sally and David a different experience of Blake's presence.

Sally, David, Alex and Nina sat around the table with an upturned glass placed at its centre. The purpose of the glass was to fuse the energy of the participants; focusing this energy so that the spirits could reach them. The four around the table closed their eyes, bowed their heads, held hands tightly and waited in silence. The sense of expectation was almost palpable and I spoke:

'Blake, Blake, can you make your presence known, please?'

I repeated these words over several minutes; the atmosphere in the room was electric. Alex was in a deep trance and opened his mouth as if to speak; his head moved slightly, as did his tongue, as he tried desperately hard to force out Blake's words. But the words were being held back.

Sally was sitting next to Alex and constantly urging Blake to speak. She spoke gently:

'Are you with us, Blake? If you are with us, will you squeeze my hand? Come on, Blake. I need to talk to you.'

But the words remained stuck in Alex's mouth. I could see him clearing his throat to speak, but the words were stuck fast.

'Blake, are you with us, we need you now,' Sally repeated.

With all our attention focused on Alex, we hadn't noticed that David had gone into a deep trance and was slumped over the table. At one point, it seemed Blake was trying to reach us through him as he, too, tried to spit out words. David was opening his mouth to speak, but the words refused to come out.

I finally broke off the séance so we could discuss it:

'A couple of times, I could feel there were things I *could* say, but I couldn't get the words out,' Alex explained. 'When I felt I wanted to say something, one of the words was "hi", but as soon as I tried to speak it, my mind took over. It was like I had a washed-over feeling.

'At one time, I suddenly felt really, really happy,' he added.

David also experienced a 'washed-over' feeling which he described thus: 'I felt cold and water coming over me, flooding over me.'

It was amazing that David had been so receptive as to feel his stepson drowning – Blake had come through to him and succeeded in communicating that.

We decided to try again. Sally, of course, was longing to speak to her son. Alex went back into a deep trance and I, again, tried to encourage Blake to come through:

'Blake,' I said, 'We've got four people here who miss you so much. Give us the affirmation that we need, climb this mountain for us. All we need is a "hi", we just need you to say "hi".'

Sally also tried again, but having come so close to making contact the atmosphere was highly charged and she found herself overwhelmed by emotion. Tears rolled down her cheeks as she gripped Alex's and David's hands, pleading, 'Please talk to us, Blake. Blake, are you there?'

Alex fell back in his chair, and David's head went down and we thought Blake was trying to talk through him but, again, no words were spoken, and we had to accept that Blake's spirit was not going to come through with any strength.

During her visits to Chamonix, Sally had befriended seventy-three-year-old Joseph Dancet. Joseph had been so moved by Sally's story that he had made it his mission to find Blake's body, even though some thought he was a crazy old man. Starting in May 2006, for eight months he raked painstakingly through tons of debris washed up by the river, sometimes sifting through three-metre deep layers of silt, rubbish and driftwood, until on 30 December that year Joseph made an incredible find.

He was walking by the river in Bonneville when, at last, he spotted a piece of bone sticking up out of the water – a miracle in itself, really – and DNA testing established that it was Blake's thigh bone. Police stuck to the supposition that Blake's death was accidental drowning.

The police divers who Sally had been promised discovered the second femur in the same area of the river. In a way, it wasn't much, but it enabled Sally to put Blake to rest at home in England and reach a degree of closure for herself. Part of Sally still wonders whether Blake fell or if he was pushed into the river that night and perhaps she always will. Sadly, the only certainty is the terrible waste of a life.

There are too many mothers and fathers in turmoil over questions that 'officials' cannot answer. That's when some families turn to mediums such as me, and to be able to help them is a privilege. Sally Perrin and Mary Kelly were fortunate in as much as their searches did reveal something tangible – each could lay her son to rest. It is the people who search in vain that I feel most sorry for; the burden of never knowing is heavy, indeed.

★ ★ ★

Despite a weak presence at the séance, Blake's spirit is certainly making himself known at Sally and David's home in Shropshire. Playing about with the electrics is a favourite with spirits – flickering lights, switching kettles on and off, messing about with the TV – I get it myself, all the time. I'll sit down to watch TV and the spirits will either put the volume on mute, or turn it full up; it's a real pain to live with sometimes.

At Sally and David's cottage, Blake sets off the burglar alarm at any hour of the day and night, which is infuriating for everyone within earshot. Naturally, the couple have had the alarm checked and double-checked, and they've been told there is no earthly reason why it should ring at random. When Sally mentioned it, I told her not to worry, 'That's just Blake letting you know he's around.'

Blake also uses the household's electrical appliances to let his mother know he is in the vicinity. This is not an uncommon way for spirits to make themselves felt: spirits are energy and electricity is energy and they seem to be able to manipulate it.

'We've had lights going off and the TV turns itself on and off,' said Sally.

'The latest thing is our smoke alarms. We've tried changing the batteries, then we even replaced them all with new ones, but they still go off. On the anniversary of Blake's death, the smoke alarms went crazy.'

* * *

On the subject of electrical phenomena, I worked on a case in which an energetic spirit made frequent use of his parents' electrical appliances to let them know he was with them. At the age of thirty-three Michael had taken his own life following the break up of his marriage. His wife, who he loved and had worshipped, left the couple's home in Hereford and, the final straw for David came when she fell pregnant – during the marriage she and David had tried unsuccessfully for a baby.

David's parents, Amanda and Jim, loved their son very much and they call me every six months or so for a telephone reading.

I first met them in Dundee early in 2007 and David came straight through. I recognized his distinctive accent and I heard and felt what had happened to him, chapter and verse:

'I can see an all terrain vehicle and fumes, why is that?' I asked Amanda and Jim.

In fact, it was the ATV which Michael would ride around the farm on. He had a lot of fun on it and he chose to die on it. He locked himself in the garage, switched on the engine and died as a result of carbon monoxide poisoning.

'I'm so sorry,' I told his parents. 'Michael was absolutely determined to take his own life, nothing would have stopped him. He slipped away quietly.

'Michael is telling me that he went home that last afternoon to an empty house, and with the prospect of Christmas and not having his wife around he just couldn't handle it any more. There was nothing you could have done to stop him.'

Michael had worked with his father as a carpenter. The family had been a close-knit one and his parents had done their best to help him recover from his broken marriage, while he tried hard to pick up the pieces of his life. But he was a broken man, totally devastated by his wife's rejection of him.

I was reading for his parents recently on the phone when Michael told me about a new car. When I asked why this would be, a very surprised Jim said he and Amanda had just bought a new car. Michael also asked me to tell his dad to 'watch his pennies'. He knew his father liked spending money and had frittered away lots of cash on cars in his youth. Now, Michael was warning him to be more cautious with his spending; typical of a Scotsman.

When I read for Amanda and Jim I often see Michael in the kitchen, 'I keep playing with the kettle,' he tells me. And, boy, does he play with that kettle. Amanda explained that Michael had always been 'very homely' and spent a lot of time with her in the kitchen. She is quite accustomed to his antics these days:

'I don't sleep well, so I often sit up after Jim's gone to

bed, until I am very tired. Michael will be up to his old tricks – flicking the kitchen light on and off and switching the kettle on to boil.

'He's tampering with the television, too, distorting the picture. He generally turns up when I'm alone, late in the evening, and it's a comfort knowing he is close. I've got used to it now. I smile and say, "Michael, you are tampering with the television again."'

I have explained to his parents that, though he is no longer on this plane, Michael wants to let them know he is still close by, and messing with these various gadgets is his way of communicating that to them. Amanda has also felt Michael's spirit touch her. When she is tearful and missing him with all her heart, he will reach out and comfort her. Alone in her sitting room one night, she felt Michael stroke the top of her head.

It is quite common for spirits to stroke the head, or even pat the shoulder, of those who mourn them on the earth plane. Blake and Michael, and others like them, are glad their families can feel their presence, and knowing such spirits are around brings peace and comfort.

Lives Barely Lived

I am always moved by those who die young, and by the pain and suffering I see in the families who come to me seeking some kind of solace. There's something particularly tragic about seeing young children taken away from their families when they still have their whole lives ahead of them. It must be heartbreaking for a parent to realize that they will never see the child who they have cared for and cherished go to school, marry or have children of their own. Though it never fails to upset me to see people in this position, it is at least some kind of consolation that my gift gives me the opportunity to relieve their suffering and even in some cases to actually provide practical help. One such case was six-year-old Daniel Palmer who introduced himself in an unforgettable way. 'My name is Daniel, D.A.N.I.E.L.,' he spelled, letter by letter, precisely as he'd been accustomed to when he was alive. Daniel wanted to make certain I knew how to spell his name.

In August 2002, Daniel had been knocked off his bicycle and killed in a hit and run accident. Almost two years on, the killer had yet to be identified and the child's parents, Luke Palmer and Vicky Murray, asked me to help track down the man who left their son to die in the road. Multiple appeals for information by police and the charity Crimestoppers had drawn a blank, despite a reward totalling £55,000 including a £30,000 pledge from Virgin boss Sir Richard Branson.

Luke and Vicky were relying on me to find some fresh clues when we met at their home. I promised to do my best to get justice for Daniel and said:

'Just take me to the road where the accident happened, tell me nothing and I will let you know what I discover.'

We were joined by two policemen, one of whom took me to the scene of the accident, just yards from Daniel's home. When he stopped, I pointed to the other end of the street and told him, 'I don't know why you are stopping here when we need to be down there.' Was he trying to trick me? Regardless, I knew this was the wrong location and let my psychic feelings lead me to where the accident had happened. Luke confirmed as correct the site I indicated.

I knew nothing about the accident other than that Daniel

had been killed on the road and the driver had failed to stop. It was as I stood on the spot where it happened that I heard Daniel spell out his name. I saw a blond-haired boy riding his shiny bicycle, having fun out playing with his friends. He then showed me what happened seconds before the crash; vivid images flashed inside my head. Daniel had come off the pavement and his bike was rocking from side to side as he rode across the road. When I asked Luke why the bike was rocking he told me, with a tear in his eye, that, 'There was a stabilizer missing and he used to rock on it.'

Jagna chipped in alongside Daniel and showed me a car speeding along the road. I then saw the crash and the driver taking a look in his rear-view mirror at Daniel lying motionless, critically injured, on the road next to his crushed bike. I saw him speed off without showing any concern for the helpless child. The driver's callous and selfish actions enraged me and I wanted to help the police find him so this family could have the justice they deserved.

Jagna told me the name of the driver which I passed on to the two policemen. I also gave them the colour and make of the vehicle I felt was involved. Daniel's parents looked at each other with fresh hope in their eyes. Without any shadow of doubt in my mind I believed the car was a blue Vauxhall Corsa.

'That's not possible,' Luke told me. 'The police think it

was a white van. They have been looking for the driver of a white van for the past two years.'

'No, that's wrong,' I said. 'I promise you it was a blue Vauxhall Corsa.'

One of the policemen came over and asked me about the car and I repeated what I'd told Luke. The policemen took a file of papers from their car and flicked through the accident case report. The report included photographs of four cars on the road at the time of the accident: one was a white van – the van they thought was responsible – but there was also a blue Vauxhall Corsa.

Unfortunately, I told the grieving parents, the killer would never be caught because he had disposed of his car in a crusher; knowing the driver's name would be useless without any evidence. It was sad, but true. The police followed up what I said and even questioned the driver I'd identified, but they couldn't make an arrest because of lack of evidence. He had got away with it and I felt so desperately sorry for Daniel's parents.

Grandparents John and Margaret Stevens contacted me through *Woman's Own* magazine, seeking reassurance following the death of their beloved granddaughter Abigail at the age of fourteen. Abigail and her best friend were killed on a level crossing. I remembered reading about the terrible accident in the press. The girls' deaths had touched hearts all over the country – they had been going into town to do some Christmas shopping.

'I've got the Pink Girl with me,' I told Margaret. 'She's telling me how she loved to wear pink.'

Abigail's nickname was the Pink Girl and, indeed, in the pictures in my head she was wearing her favourite colour from top to toe.

'That's her, that's our Abigail. She was always in pink,' said Margaret.

'She's telling me that she's missing her present. What does this mean?'

'I'd sent Abigail a cheque for her birthday and she was going into town to spend it with her friend on the day she was killed,' Margaret explained.

Abigail wanted me to reassure her grandmother that she was safe and that she didn't suffer when she died. She wanted me to pass on that they were in such a rush to catch the train that they hadn't looked before stepping onto the track. Then she said how very much she loved her grandmother and was so happy to be talking to her, and she also said she knew how much her family missed her. Then she had one last message for her grandparents:

'She wants to thank you for her wonderful pink funeral. She could see that everyone wore pink in her memory.'

During the reading, Abigail had said that she wanted to speak to her mother. Three months later a woman came to see me, though when I first met her I didn't know she was Abigail's mother. Abigail's spirit came through – dressed in her pink – and she was delighted to be able to speak to her mother through me:

'Tell Mum I'm glad that she is happy,' said Abigail. 'She's with a guy I know.'

Her mother and father had separated and her mother was going out with a teacher at the school her daughter had attended.

A young woman came to see me recently and her twenty-month-old daughter came through. I knew the toddler had drowned – I felt cold and water rushing over me – and I felt the confusion, the absolute confusion, which I suppose she must have felt.

I saw her wearing the most wonderful, bright pink clothes and her mother told me how much her little girl had adored the colour.

'She's holding something like a teddy, but it's not a teddy, though it's cuddly. It's the weirdest looking thing,' I said. Neither her mother nor I could figure out what it might be. I continued to try and describe what I was seeing, but I'd never seen anything like it, so all I could say was that it was weird but cuddly. Then it registered with the girl's mother and she told me it was a Makka Pakka, one of the characters from a BBC children's TV show, *In the Night Garden*.

'It was one of her favourites and she was buried with it,' she said.

I was glad to have identified that strange looking creature.

The little girl who loved Makka Pakka drowned in a swimming pool and the sensation of drowning came through very strongly. Interpreting what was happening when the son of an Irish woman came through was a little trickier.

The boy I could see was around twelve years old, and my head hurt as I experienced the sensation of water rushing over me. The boy's death seemed more to do with a head injury than drowning:

'It's really strange,' I told his mother. 'But I feel I am in water and I bang my head. I bang my head and I'm gone.'

'He was floating on a Lilo in a swimming pool in Spain. He fell off and banged his head on the floor of the pool and died,' she explained.

To love and protect their children is the most natural and important thing in the world for most parents. When a child commits suicide it is, therefore, very, very hard for the parents to accept that their child had been so unhappy that they'd taken their own life.

A mother seeking answers about her son's suicide came to me for a reading. Describing what I saw in my mind's eye of the boy's death I told her:

'I feel like I'm flying, but it's really strange because as I'm flying I can see cars. It's like I've fallen off a multistorey car park.'

'That's exactly what happened. But he didn't fall, he was pushed,' said the boy's mother.

'He tells me he was all dressed up in his best clothes and he'd splashed on some nice aftershave.'

The bereaved mother nodded agreement.

'Well, look, my love, there wasn't an altercation. He took his own life.'

'No,' she insisted. 'My son wouldn't take his own life. I'm telling you, he wouldn't do that.'

Again, I had to contradict her. I told her what her son's spirit was telling me. I didn't mean to be harsh, but I can only tell it as I see it:

'I'm so sorry, my love, but he did take his own life. He's even telling me he took his shoes off and left them on the top level.'

I'm told that it's not unusual for someone planning to jump in such circumstances to first remove their shoes. I don't know why. She concurred, her son's shoes had been found.

The reading left this mother feeling deeply disappointed, because I told her that her son committed suicide. The verdict at the inquest into his death had been suicide, too, but the boy's mother couldn't accept it. She came to me hoping I would find she was right – that her son had been pushed. I told her the truth as I saw it: that is what I do.

As I mentioned earlier, I generally don't give readings to children under the age of sixteen, but I will work on them for healing. One of the cases I am most proud of healing was Molly, a premature baby girl born at twenty-four weeks at Addenbrooke's Hospital, Cambridge, in 2005. Her father, Kevin, worked with my son and it was he, Daniel, who suggested I might be able to help – Molly had been given a five per cent chance of surviving.

When he went to visit Molly at Addenbrooke's that night, Kevin told his partner, Julia, about me and she phoned, pleading with me to come straight away because, 'We are desperate and you're our last resort.' The hospital was no more than a twenty-minute drive from my home, so I soon arrived at the Rosie Maternity Unit and followed Julia into a ward full of sick babies in incubators. I looked down at the little bundle that was Molly; she was the tiniest baby I have ever seen and she looked so fragile.

Molly's early arrival in the world meant she was born with underdeveloped lungs and a hole in her heart, plus she was battling with a bowel disease. She was in one of the best hospitals in the country and receiving the best care possible, yet her chances were poor. It was one heck of a challenge.

'She is the most beautiful baby I have ever seen. I can tell she is a fighter,' I told her parents.

'I am going to place my hands above her organs and let the energy come through to do the healing. I can feel her lungs are not formed right. I am going to connect to my spirit guides who will work through me. They will send their energy through me.'

I closed my eyes and focused hard to connect with Jagna and White Cloud. I concentrated hard on Molly's lungs and bowel, then placed my hands a couple of inches above her chest. My hands started tingling and became very warm – the powerful energies were going through me. I hoped desperately this healing would help.

When I returned the following day to repeat the healing, a group of doctors and nurses watched what I did without comment. I made five or six visits to the hospital and, miraculously, Molly pulled through; she is four years old now, she's healthy and she is absolutely lovely.

Julia is a nurse and she's adamant that, alongside all the specialist medical treatment, my healing hands played a part in her daughter's survival. She was, as she said, 'desperate' when she called and I'm glad to have been there for her and Kevin and Molly in their hour of need.

Epilogue

When I was younger I never really knew what my gift was for. Even as I got older and learnt more and more about it, I still struggled to work out why I of all people had been given this ability to talk to the other side, to see the future and tell others things about themselves even they had no way of knowing. How would things have turned out for me if I'd been born just like my brothers, like any normal boy? A psychic ability isn't just a switch you can flick on and off; it's no exaggeration to say that it takes over your life, so it's not like it's something I could have just forgotten, or brought out once in a while like a party trick. Inevitably it made me wonder what was in it for me. The way I once saw it, a gift wasn't really a gift unless you got something out of it yourself. Mine only seemed to make demands on me – sometimes it's hard not to see it as a bit of a burden.

I brought it up with White Cloud once, but his reaction told me in no uncertain terms that it wasn't something he was willing to discuss. Blunt as she is, Jagna, I knew, would give me even shorter shrift, so I never even tried with her. Nevertheless, it was something that nagged at me for years. I'm not saying that it was always on my mind; for one thing I was much too busy to have any time to get lost in self-pity, and to be honest, wallowing's not really my thing. But, occasionally, dog-tired after a long day, driving home by myself, there it would be. Why am I doing this? What is it all for?

It was when I visited the Wellses that second time, seeing the relief I brought them after having passed on Holly's words, that I began to realize what it was actually all about. This gift wasn't really for me. Sure, it acted through me, and I was the one that Jagna and White Cloud spoke to, but I was fooling myself if I thought I was anything more than a medium for something else totally outside what I could ever comprehend. I was simply a vehicle for something huge, something none of us will ever really understand or make sense of. But it was seeing this that brought home to me how lucky I was. I have the ability to do something for others that no amount of money, education or hard work could bring them. Of course, it is devastating, telling someone their child has died, or being the one to extinguish the last spark of hope in a grieving wife's eyes;

those things are never going to be easy. My gift has also shown me things that I pray God nobody else will ever have to see. I will never forget those awful few moments when to all intents and purposes I *was* BTK; believe me, I wouldn't wish that on even my own worst enemy. Against that though is the good I have been able to do, and I don't think I'm being big headed if I say that I've been given the chance to carry out more than my fair share – it still gives me the most unbelievable buzz.

And in a way, that leads me to the great thing that my gift *has* done for me. It hasn't brought me riches or showed me an easy path to happiness, though at times I've wished for both, but it has made me a better person. That's not to say I was a bad man before, I like to think that, for all my rough edges, I've always been a pretty decent bloke. However, there's a side to me now that people years ago, when I was the kind of man who settled arguments with a swing of my fist, would never have guessed I possessed. Call it what you will, a more feminine side, a new sensitivity, but I'm much more in touch with my feelings, much better at expressing them openly than I was back in the days when I was a gamekeeper. And by the same token, I now have such a strong empathy with the emotions of others, I can feel their hurt, their joy, their hope and frustrations as intensely as they would themselves. You could argue I've just mellowed with age; perhaps I have. And yet spending so much time on intimate terms with the inner lives of everyone from celebrities to widows without a stick to call their own, how could that not change me?

I like to think that in turn this has made me a better psychic, because this is what that life is all about. It's not about flashy tricks on TV or pulling the wool over some poor punter's eyes at a public demonstration; it's about doing the best you can with what you've been given, putting yourself at the service of others and knowing that helping them is in itself its own reward. Who knows, one day White Cloud or Jagna may tell me why I was given these extraordinary gifts, but for me, this is already answer enough. I have been lucky just to meet some of the men and women I've mentioned on these pages, and I hope that in telling my story, I've also written an adequate testament to their kindness, bravery and generosity. If getting to know them has been a privilege, working with them has been, and always will be, an honour.